Truth of Nagasaki:
The Remedy for Nuclear Paralysis

Truth of Nagasaki:
The Remedy for Nuclear Paralysis

Hironobu FUJIO

Truth of Nagasaki: The Remedy for Nuclear Paralysis

ISBN: 978-1-64273-359-4

Written by Hironobu FUJIO
Project Editor: Yumi Itabashi, Hachidori Inc.
Editor: Andrew Kirkham

Printed in USA
1 2 3 4 5 6 7 8 9 10

One Peace Books
43-32 22nd Street STE 204 Long Island City New York 11101
www.onepeacebooks.com

CONTENTS

FOREWORD

I wonder how the people of the world see the Japanese.

Despite being the only nation to have suffered a nuclear attack, Japan's government did not participate in the first meeting for the Treaty on the Prohibition of Nuclear Weapons—not even as an observer.

I wonder what people think the reason for that was.

Did Japan consider itself protected by the USA's nuclear umbrella?
Did Japan feel grateful to the US for facilitating its "Economic Miracle"?
Did Japan feel that it was, spiritually, under continued US occupation?

I believe that this book offers answers to such questions that at least get us closer to the truth.

The Treaty on the Prohibition of Nuclear Weapons First Meeting of States Parties this June in Vienna garnered much attention, even in Japan, and the timing was uncomfortably prescient: July 10th was Election Day for a major electoral race in the Japanese Diet, with nearly all parties advocating for greater defense expenditures in response to the COVID-19 pandemic and Russia's invasion of Ukraine, in conjunction with policies intended to stimulate the economy. However, not a soul, candidate or citizen, spoke out with commitment for abolishing nuclear weapons.

I am a physician, and I find this situation to be deeply concerning. In the course of my work as a general practitioner, being engaged day-in and day-out with patients of all ages as I seek diagnoses, treatments, and cures for my patients' ills—be they infectious, chronic, cancerous, or mental—I have engaged with numerous people who directly experienced World War II. The interactions I have had with such patients, supported by my consultation of over 100 other texts of relevant literature, are the foundation upon which I wrote this book.

As a physician in the only country to have ever suffered a nuclear strike, I published a book named 'Revive The Bells of Nagasaki!' in Japan. I believe that I have a unique duty to convey my findings to the world. I have now written a new book based on this book and translated it into English. **I hope that translations of this work will find its proper audience, and that you, the reader, will learn something from what I have written.**

My wife is also a physician and works tirelessly for the benefit of her patients. We both have busy lives, but one of our little joys is eating dinner together at a German restaurant in the neighborhood of our home, a live-in clinic.

Recently, when we were having dinner at this restaurant, a friend and fellow regular customer–our notably erudite local postmaster–said to us that he finds something suspicious about the two-party system of the USA. He said something along these lines: "Hironobu, many of the Presidents who have been engaged with nuclear weapons in some fashion have belonged to the Democratic Party. For example, FDR and the Manhattan Project, Truman and the dropping of Little Boy and Fat Man, Kennedy and the Cuban missile crisis, and even Obama with his presidential visit to Hiroshima. In comparison, many Republican presidents, such as Bush, Reagan, and Trump, have merely focused on trying to strengthen the economy."

I am in no position to judge whether or not this is a reasonable position. However, in the course of writing this book, I have found that there remains much about America that I would like to better understand.

Nonetheless, there is one thing that I believe that I can say. The vast majority of Japanese people, if asked if it would have been better for the USSR or the USA to occupy Japan following our defeat in World War II, would say "America."

I wish for this America—the America that the Japanese people have chosen to trust—to abolish their nuclear arsenal. Let this new America work together with Japan to create truly beautiful, prosperous nations of the future. This is my heartfelt desire.

1. THE A-BOMBED DUTCHMAN

A certain "Dr. M" gained high marks in the former Kokura Middle School, sufficient to enter a high school for elite students near the Nagasaki area. He was an artistic youth who loved Schubert and Beethoven, able to sing a German lied in the original language by age 18. Despite English, at the time, being viewed as the "language of the enemy" that most were forbidden to use, it was available at his high school, and he studied it—along with classes on electricity, mechanical engineering, civil engineering, and architecture.

At the time, America was in control of Okinawa, and the outcome of the Pacific Theater of WWII was coming into view. Nonetheless, the Japanese army refused to accept defeat and continued to pursue active engagement, with a draft so aggressive that manufacturing industries, already struggling to re-tool their factories for weapons manufacture, became understaffed. Dr. M, along with around 100 of his classmates, ended up being pushed into working in a war plant in Nagasaki. This war plant was none other than Mitsubishi Heavy Industry's massive Nagasaki Shipyard that produced, at the time, the largest battleship in history: Battleship Musashi. Dr. M's role at the plant was in building the hulls of the Kaiten suicide-bomb mini-submarines, adapted from torpedo architecture.

This shipyard, which produced a large number of warships aside from Battleship Musashi, would naturally have been tactically focused on undermining the US military position. At the time, control of the airspace had been almost entirely lost; Dr. M recounted a sense of being constantly seized with the fear that an airstrike on the shipyard was imminent. Had the US forces been so inclined, it would have been a straightforward task for them to deploy airborne pressure from their carriers in the coastal waters of Japan to destroy the extra-large cranes and docks and other facilities that enabled the construction of the 60-kiloton ships like the Musashi.

August 9, 1945

On this day, the hot rays of summer shone bright from early morning, and the calm waters of Nagasaki Bay offered no foreshadow. Dr. M emerged from his lodging in Kogakura, located on the far shore from the war plant, and boarded a ferry some 50 tons in size from a local port. The journey took a mere half-hour, but in the company of the cries of lazy seabirds, soaring this way and that, it was a striking little trip along the coast.

After Dr. M disembarked, he reported to his block in the Mitsubishi Shipyard at 10 AM and began his work: welding curved **"rain-bucket-type"** steel plates together to craft the hulls of the one-man suicide bomber submarines. As he was doing so, an air-raid alarm began blaring, and he hurried to a nearby bomb shelter. However, the alarm was called off 30 minutes later. In a state of bewitched stupor, he left the bomb shelter, where he saw, off in the distance, a B-29 Superfortress drifting in the blue sky. Disturbed and disheartened that there appeared to be no friendly forces en-route to intercept it, Dr. M returned to his work.

Shortly thereafter, Dr. M took a break to use the toilet, by which time the B-29 he saw just a few minutes before was no longer visible. Instead, he saw a white parachute hanging in the sky to the north (in retrospect, he realized that this was the surveillance device deployed by the consort plane, along with the bomb, for gathering data on the drop).

About when he thought that it was already 11, he took off his welding visor and looked towards the sun. At that very moment, he recounts seeing an indescribable flash of intensely bright light and a rapidly expanding donut-shaped ring of pink-tinged orange. As he had never seen anything remotely like this before, his first thought was that some kind of unheard-of accident had taken place elsewhere in the shipyard, and instinctively threw himself down to take shelter. Just at that moment, the searing blast of the explosion caught up with him, sending him hurtling across the ground. Luckily, his injuries from the incident were relatively minor, and he was able to quickly stand up and make his way to the bomb shelter.

Only five workers from other sections had managed to make it to the bomb shelter. One of them was yelling that the air-raid was one of the special large-scale bombs. In fact, the papers had reported on the novel bomb that the US military had dropped on Hiroshima 3 days earlier, but not enough time had yet passed to confirm that it was a nuclear explosion. The previously blue sky was, by then, obscured with an ashen haze, and to the north at ground zero, a strange, jellyfish-like cumulonimbus cloud was reaching higher and higher.

After leaving the bomb shelter and returning to their station, those workers who survived spent hours in silence as they toiled on the 2-meter-wide small-type submarines, gripped by a fear and uncertainty they had never before experienced, uncertain of what kind of calamity might befall them next.

In the early afternoon on that day, black rain came sprinkling down, staining the workers' white jumpsuits with countless black dots. As ground zero was 6 kilometers away, there didn't appear to be any particularly devastating damage, and the functionality of metal structures such as the ferries and things in the harbor remained intact. Dr. M fearfully made his return trip to Kogakura, only to find that his dormitory, a much flimsier structure of wood, had suffered extensive damage, exposing him to the wind and rain. However, with no other lodging option available, he had no choice but to endure it.

Dr. M, along with his coworkers, soon received orders from their superior. They were to offer relief to the victims of the devastation that befell the Nagasaki city center due to the bombing–so off they went, hardtack rations in tow.

After I heard this story from Dr. M, who was nearly 90 years of age, I asked him what the city center was like after the bombing. He did not answer, but instead stared off into the distance with a vague expression, silent. This question may not have recalled hardtack biscuits to his mind, so much as groaning pleas for "Water! Water!" from men, women, and children, bodies raw in disfigurement from the explosion. Undying eyes, lips, tongues, blistered from extreme heat, writhing like giant leeches. The vision of suffering must have been horrendous. The stench of innumerable corpses would already have been oppressively inescapable anywhere survivors still remained. Arms, legs, and heads, charred to a hideous black, scattered everywhere. Faces contorted into expressions of anguish like grotesque curios, eyes forever staring, as if in accusation of some unknown force. I felt as though the images that must have flooded his mind at that moment had briefly been projected into mine. Undoubtedly, he has tried to seal them away and forget those memories. I decided not to ask him about the matter a second time.

However, he was willing to tell me about an encounter he had with an enemy Dutch soldier on his march to Nagasaki after receiving his order to transport the hardtack rations. Dr. M's wife, who was also present at the time, reacted as though she had never heard this story before. I wonder if, thinking that he had little time left, Dr. M decided that he could share this one story with me.

That Dutch soldier was being held at a POW camp, but being close to ground zero, the building had been destroyed, effectively making him a free man. Chances where that he had suffered harsh treatment while he was imprisoned. Nonetheless, the intense cruelty and tragedy of what remained after the bombing may have left him dumbfounded and robbed him of his motivation to flee, resulting in his meeting with Dr. M as he wandered aimlessly.

The two young men were able to connect through English and German, and for a while, the soldier aided him as a volunteer in distributing the hardtack. However, what the victims wanted most after the bombing was water. Almost nobody was interested in the hardtack, so the two of them ended up using the rations to address their own hunger. Dr. M said, "You know, that Dutch soldier was telling me how inhumane the Japanese POW camp was, that they were being forced to eat tree roots and the like. So, I told him, I'm pretty sure that was just burdock root, Japanese people eat that all the time, and in Grimm's fairy tales, there are also stories where people are eating root vegetables." I have no idea whether or not anyone eats root vegetables in Grimm's fairy tales. However, I get the impression that these two, in spite of the hair-raising horror of their surroundings, had managed to create a moment–if only a moment–of human levity together.

After 150 years of constant civil war, by 1600, Tokugawa Ieyasu had become the 'Shogun' and unified Japan. That unifying government was labeled the *Edo-bakufu* (Edo shogunate), and subsequent generations of leaders were always selected from within the Tokugawa family. The Edo shogunate embraced an exclusionary policy towards foreign trade, known as *sakoku* (literally, "chained country"), but the single port of Nagasaki was permitted to proactively engage in trade with the Dutch. As a result, until the collapse of the Edo shogunate in 1868 and subsequent changes in policy, Nagasaki was Japan's sole window into the West and mediated almost entirely by the Dutch.

I wonder if it would be reasonable to view Dr. M's encounter with the Dutch soldier at Nagasaki as an echo of this rich history. Afterwards, Dr. M would go on to graduate from Kyushu University's School of Medicine, and after he completed training as an internalist, succeeded his father's clinic in Kokura, where he continued a tradition of honest medical practice. While he long kept the details of what he saw at ground-zero Nagasaki to himself, he reflected daily on the immeasurable value of life. Eventually, he was nominated to a prestigious position as the head of his regional medical association, and also acted as a mediator and manager for fellow private practitioners. However, his experiences at Nagasaki led to his opposition of the construction of the nuclear power plants that were being advocated by the Liberal Democratic Party of Japan (also known as Jimintō) - the party that his medical association supported. As a result, after he left his position as the association's head, he announced his refusal to support that party. And now, at 90 years of age and 30 years my senior, he was telling me stories of the horrors of the Nagasaki bombing with matter-of-fact detachment, surrounded by the beautifully blossoming flowers he grows in his hobby as a gardener.

Even though it had built Battleship Musashi, the largest warship in history, the famed Mitsubishi Heavy Industries Nagasaki Shipyard had emerged from the bombing with barely a scratch. From a tactical perspective, one would expect a military to target a military facility that is producing warships. Why, then, was Urakami, a heavily populated civilian center, selected for the bombing?

After WWII, the Nagasaki Shipyard became active again around the time of the Korean War, using its advanced technological capabilities to construct super tankers, passenger ships, and the like. I once went on a cruise with my wife on the Motor Ship Asuka II, which was also built at Nagasaki. The Asuka II is a beautiful ship, and I would like to ride it again someday.

However, aside from civilian vessels, the Nagasaki Shipyard also produces a large number of ships for Japan's Maritime Self Defense Forces. What exactly does that mean? To be clear, right now, it is acting at the behest of the Japanese government–and under the protection of the US nuclear umbrella–to build up Japan's defensive capabilities. What are we to make of a situation like this?

First, let's go on a journey. A journey to the depths of Nagasaki, ground zero.

2. THE FIRST TARGET

"Man, we sure are lucky that the A-bomb wasn't dropped on Kokura!"

So exclaimed Iccho Itoh, the former mayor of Nagasaki, when he saw "Kokura" on my clinic's business card. As these words rang out, a sudden tension ripped through the reception hall, filled with over 200 guests.

This happened in November of 2003, at the Nagasaki Global Citizens' Assembly for the Elimination of Nuclear Weapons.

In the moment, Mr. Itoh's eyes went wide, with an expression of both anger and sadness. He yelled this out with deep emotion, as though he had encountered a once-in-a-lifetime opportunity to make a declaration to the world. The people who were gathered around the former mayor watched for my reaction with astonished, uncertain smiles.

I felt like I had been punched in the stomach, and I can't remember what I said in response, but Mr. Itoh immediately resumed friendly conversation with others as though nothing had just occurred.

According to an announcement by the US military, the intended target of the nuclear bombing on August 9, 1945 was Kokura (now registered as Kokurakita Ward in the city of Kitakyushu). However, because of cloud cover in the area above the target, visual confirmation for the drop was severely impaired. Nonetheless, three runs were made in the effort to carry out the drop. Due to an assessment that anti-air fire from the Japanese military was too intense and enemy fighter aircraft were en-route to engage, and because fuel was running low, the first target was reluctantly abandoned in favor of the second target

—Nagasaki. Supposedly, the bomb ended up drifting far from the original target point in, ultimately detonating near Urakami Cathedral.

This narrative is now generally accepted as "fact" by most people.

Regardless, I don't imagine that Mr. Itoh ever met anyone from Kokura that sarcastically proclaimed, "We sure are lucky the bomb wasn't dropped on Kokura!" I think it's understandable if citizens to express their frustration and anger in private by questioning why was the bomb dropped on Nagasaki and not Kokura. However, if a mayor who represents 400,000 people were to say something like this as a public remark, I imagine it would be quite controversial.

I got the impression that Mr. Itoh just blurted this out when he met me without thinking. It was as though he was making an emotional plea specifically to me, who came from "First Target Kokura," to absorb some of his frustration. Maybe there was some kind of aura about me that triggered this reaction in him.

I was introduced to Mr. Itoh by Dr. David Krieger, a consultant for the Global Citizen's Assembly. He witnessed this exchange, but it seemed like he didn't understand what had happened. He was a friend of mine and the president of the Nuclear Age Peace Foundation, but at the time, he was unaware of the famous announcement that declared Kokura to be the first intended target for the second nuclear bomb. He established the Nuclear Age Peace Foundation in 1982, and by 2003, he would have had accumulated significant experience with bomb victims and nuclear weapon abolitionists in Nagasaki. None of those people in Nagasaki had ever grievously complained to him that Kokura was the first target, but that the bomb was dropped on Nagasaki instead.

After being spoken to in this shocking manner by the former mayor, and with my friend Dr. Krieger–who was the only person I knew at the event–not understanding why it was such an upsetting statement, I felt even more alone. There were about 200 attendees at the reception. I was initially unable to relinquish my sense of isolation in that environment, but after talking to a number of bomb victims in attendance, I began to feel more like myself again. One older man with an honest-looking face said to me, in a friendly way, "Oh, you're from Kokura? Thank you for coming all this way, it's a pleasure to meet you. I got caught in the explosion and was hurt pretty badly, yet I've managed to live this long. The truth is, I was just given a second chance, even though my health hasn't always been so good. I'm surprised I'm still around, myself! It's thanks to my friends, who died in the blast. I think they let me live on, asking me to stick around for their sake."

I felt so lost and out of place after being told that I was lucky that my hometown wasn't the one that was bombed, but this kindly old man's words purified my heart in an instant. Not long after, Mr. Itoh came up to me. With passion, he said to me, "There's something that I want to say to you, being a visitor from Kokura. Nagasaki and Kokura have had deep ties since the Edo Period (1603), being connected by the Nagasaki Road (*Nagasaki kaidō*). The importance of our shared history is not lost on me. I want the people of Kokura to think more deeply about the bombing we suffered. I truly hope that in so doing, we can restore our old relations." The look in his eyes as he said this was so full of sincerity, and it has been scorched into my memory ever since.

Former Mayor Itoh's view could be summarized as follows:

1. The people of Nagasaki believe it is the responsibility of Kokura to mend relations between Kokura and the bomb victims.
2. The people of Kokura do not think about the bombing of Nagasaki very seriously. The true "intended" target for the nuclear strike on August 9, 1945 was Kokura!

The Nagasaki Atomic Bomb Museum also presents this narrative as fact. I recall being in the museum and being astounded when I overheard an old woman reading about it exclaim, "Nagasaki was so unlucky!"

If it is true that Kokura had managed to escape a nuclear strike, then certainly, some good luck was involved. If the people of Kokura had made a single misstep, they may have met the same tragic fate that befell Nagasaki. Sometimes it seems as though the people of Kokura don't quite grasp this reality.

However, after many years of living in Kokura, I think there is some nuance missing here.

When this topic is brought up in Kokura, it is quite common for people to suddenly lower their voices and speak in a different tone, and avoid staying on the subject for very long. When confronted with the overwhelming reality of the bombing, people tend to reveal their sentiments that they were indeed lucky, that they feel guilty, or that they have to find some way to show gratitude to Nagasaki. As a result, they try to avoid the topic altogether.

In August of every year, the Kitakyushu municipal government releases a newsletter that discusses the second bombing. The contents change every year, but the importance of remembering that Kokura was the first target and the importance of cherishing peace are common themes. That said, these missives never become major points of discussion in the Kokura public discourse.

3. HIROSHIMA, KOKURA, NAGASAKI

World War II ended with Japan's unconditional surrender on August 15, 1945.

During the US occupation, the development of aircraft and large-scale battleships was kept under tight control. This was because, during WWII, Japan had produced a string of technological breakthroughs in its development of fighter aircraft (such as the Zero fighter), large-scale battleships, submarines, aircraft carriers, and the like.

Notably, the Battleships Yamato and Musashi remain the largest battleships ever built in history. Whether or not this is because this style of military vessel fell out of favor with the changing time, the fact remains. After the war, the hulls of three of the I-400-class submarines developed in the waning years of the conflict were studied in detail before being destroyed; the design concept of these submarines ended up being employed in the development of the nuclear submarines that ran rampant in the depths of the oceans during the Cold War.

The Nakajima Ki-84 *Hayate* aircraft and others, similarly developed in the final years of WWII, were surprisingly capable despite running on poor-quality Japanese gasoline. When these planes were flown with high-quality American gasoline after the war, they proved able to fly at nearly 700 kilometers an hour, rivaling the fastest American aircraft at the time.

It was on this basis that the US was faced with a dilemma: if Japan was permitted to continue to use its industrial technological prowess to develop weapons of war, a revitalized Japanese air force of the future might eventually surpass American technology, seriously threatening US plans for global hegemony. Consequently, after the war, the US Occupation Forces forbade the development of jet planes and large-scale warships, redirecting Japan's machine industry towards peace-time industries: trains, transport ships, automobiles. One consequence of this was the development of the *Shinkansen*, considered to be the fastest train in the world, which has a network all throughout Japan, with Tokyo at the center.

Let's use the Shinkansen network as a way to explain the relationships between the major locations in this book: Hiroshima, Kokura, and Nagasaki.

From Tokyo, which is located in the center of Honshu, the largest of the four main islands of Japan, the 480 kilometer journey to Kyoto on the fastest west-bound Shinkansen train (which has a top speed of about 300 km/h) takes 2 hours and 15 minutes. Another 240 kilometers west, a passenger can reach Hiroshima in another 1 hour and 35 minutes. West from Hiroshima, the Kanmon Strait that separates Honshu and Kyushu necessitates passage by an undersea tunnel, on the other side of which is Kokura: the welcome gate to Kyushu. This journey is about 190 kilometers in distance, and on a non-stop train, takes another 47 minutes. There is currently no Shinkansen service from Kokura to Nagasaki, but if this route is built, it would be about 200 kilometers in length; the journey would probably take a little over an hour on the express line.

While the Shinkansen is capable of reaching speeds of 300 km/h, when the many turns that the geography requires and various en-route stops are considered, it is clear why the top speed of the train would not be in direct proportion with the distance travelled.

The patrol speed of the B-29 is said to have been about 350 km/h. It would likely take this aircraft about half the time of the Shinkansen to fly a direct path between each of these cities.

Now let's return to the topic of Kokura.

Kokura is now a ward in the center of the city of Kitakyushu, which, being on the northern tip of Kyushu, is the gate to the island from Honshu. As mentioned previously, it is roughly equidistant from Nagasaki and Hiroshima.

There is little traffic here. Land is cheap and the food is good. The urban center is blessed with a rich topography: both mountains and ocean are only a short distance away. The medical institutions are robust, and care for the elderly is well-funded. The people of Kokura are open-minded and honest, life is comfortable, and while I personally am from the nearby city of Fukuoka, which is the largest city on Kyushu Island, it has been more than 30 years since I moved here. Kitakyushu, the city that contains Kokura, has repeatedly taken first place in the "Top Three City Nightscapes of Japan" ranking, with its residents being able to boast of a number of spots with great night views near them no matter where they live.

There are also quite a few famous Japanese restaurants in Kokura. The quality of the seafood in particular is well-known. And, as I mentioned before, there's a German restaurant near me where my wife and I frequently eat dinner together as a small break from our busy lives as doctors. We also eat at the sushi restaurants and Mediterranean restaurants that are popular with people from the nearby Kyushu Dental College. Like many other Japanese cities, there is also a castle in the middle of it that was built long ago. There is a stylish Italian restaurant located next to the castle that we like to visit as well.

West from Kokura Station, after passing through a bustling sort of area, the Murasaki River comes into view. Further on is the region containing City Hall and Kokura Castle, an expansive commercial area with wide promenades and beautiful views, with the rolling, lush greens of Katsuyama Park at its center. The origin point of the old Nagasaki Road is also in this area. The Kitakyushu Performing Arts Center is located near Kokura Castle, and for a time, my wife and I pursued our singing hobby as dual vocalists at a concert sponsored by our clinic that was held there every year, where we could perform with some truly talented musicians. The main reason for us to choose this venue was how it offered reverberant acoustics in the midst of beautiful scenery. Our concerts always ended with an audience full of happy faces.

Enshrined in one part of Katsuyama Park is the Atomic Bomb Victim Peace Memorial and the Bell of Nagasaki, which together are a place for the people of Kokura to offer prayers.

There, an inscription reads as follows:

> "This area once held a military arsenal. US forces, seeking to bomb it, flew a plane carrying a nuclear bomb over Kokura, but due to cloud cover, changed their target to Nagasaki, upon which they dropped that same weapon. Reflecting upon this history, this memorial is established for the people of Kitakyushu to offer their earnest prayers for peace, and to offer consolation for the souls of the lives lost in the nuclear attack.
> August 9, 1973"

The following is written on the pedestal above which the Bell of Nagasaki hangs:

> "The Bell of Nagasaki (ANGELUS) was a bell meant to celebrate the Annunciation of the Virgin Mary, which hung in the old Urakami Cathedral. There were originally two, one in each of two towers of the cathedral, but one was destroyed in the explosion from the nuclear bomb dropped on August 9, 1945. The other was recovered from the debris on December 24 of the same year, and was dubbed the "Bell of Nagasaki" by Dr. Takashi Nagai, **a Catholic physician who survived the bombing.**
> After the war, Kitakyushu established the Atomic Bomb Victim Peace Memorial in Katsuyama Park to honor the souls of the bomb victims. In recognition of the cities' shared bond, Nagasaki presented Kitakyushu with a replica of the Bell of Nagasaki in the August of 1976."

"The Bells of Nagasaki" is a non-fiction account that begins a few days before the second atomic bombing on August 9, 1945 and continues until Christmas, 1945. The author, Dr. Takashi Nagai was a 37-year-old radiologist at Nagasaki Medical College Hospital when the atomic bomb was detonated. (The Bells of Nagasaki, Editorial Preface)

The Bell of Nagasaki in Katsuyama Park is itself a replica of the bell that was given by Nagasaki; the original replica is kept safely in the front entrance lobby of Kitakyushu City Hall.

Kitakyushu City Hall is a 15-story building located between Kokura Castle and Murasaki River that comes into view after a 10-minute walk from the memorial. The building towers over the loose urban scenery that surrounds it, and upon entering, the Bell of Nagasaki is on display to the left. Next to it is the Kitakyushu Anti-Nuclear Municipality for Peace Declaration of February 10, 2010. It states the following:

> "We, the people of Kitakyushu, in our somber recognition of Kokura as the initial target of the nuclear bomb that devastated Nagasaki, hereby declare our dedication to teaching future generations the horror of nuclear weapons and the tragedies of war, and to building a peaceful world free of both nuclear weaponry and warfare."

This same lobby, acting as the "face" of Kitakyushu, also contains a fan area for Giravanz Kitakyushu, a soccer team followed by Kitakyushu officials and citizens alike, as well as an exhibition on the Yahata Steel Works, which once was a highly esteemed pillar of Japan's development that was the foundation of the current municipality. In other words, Kitakyushu considers the Nagasaki bombing one of the top three most-defining things about the city, and the administration, at the very least, has long emphasized the importance of the bombing.

Despite this, when I met former Mayor Itoh, he said that he wants the people of Kokura to take the bombing of Nagasaki more seriously. I think I understand what he truly meant by this, however: no matter how much the government may promote the issue, the reaction from the city's residents at large remains lackluster.

This was only my first meeting with Mr. Itoh, so why did he saddle me with these emotions? True, they are a deep undercurrent of the Nagasaki psyche and likely lack a good outlet, but I remain unsure.

Until his unexpected death, I never spoke about this incident to anyone except my closest friends. I never thought there would come a day that I would write about it. After all, an active mayor of Nagasaki had made a sarcastic remark in a public venue about Kokura not actually getting bombed. This is extreme language–and it concerned the lives and deaths of hundreds of thousands of people.

Nonetheless, I will never, ever forget the force of his voice and the deep mix of anger, sadness, hope, and encouragement that I heard and saw in what he said to me.

4. THE NAGASAKI ROAD: STRAIGHT FROM KOKURA TO NAGASAKI

After 150 years of constant civil war, Toyotomi Hideyoshi brought Japan together in 1583. Claiming it to be necessary for political stability, he ordered 26 Catholics to be crucified in Nagasaki, the city that had seen the greatest amount of conversion by that time. After the death of Hideyoshi, Tokugawa Ieyasu established the Edo shogunate in Edo (now Tokyo) in 1603; during a power struggle in 1615, he ordered the execution of the descendants of Hideyoshi, who had been his biggest rival. As a result, Ieyasu's position as the supreme ruler of Japan was firmly established. This resulted in a strong national polity defined by a unified administration. The Edo period's feudal system of shogunate and fiefdoms lasted for 15 generations, headed by Ieyasu's own descendants, and was a time of ongoing peace during which every aspect of Japanese culture blossomed. Under this system, the Edo shogunate, headed by the shogun, was the center of government, with other areas of Japan separated into fiefdoms that were administered by feudal lords appointed by the shogun.

At the outset, the Edo shogunate sought to mend its dilapidated relations with China and Korea by adopting good-neighbor policies meant to encourage trade, designating Nagasaki for international commerce, while adopting protectionist policies in response to the arrival of ships from Portugal, Spain, the Netherlands, and England.

Meanwhile, after the Jesuit Francis Xavier (1506–1552) began a Christian mission in Japan, there were purportedly 750,000 followers of the religion throughout Japan by 1605. In response, the Edo shogunate increasingly began seeing Japanese Christians as a threat to the authority of their newly established system. The reason for this was the administration's awareness of the close relationship between the missionaries' activities and the colonialist behavior of Portugal and Spain. The administration was also seriously concerned about the possibility of the Christian faith taking deep root among the people, eventually leading to claims from powerful converts against the legitimacy of the shogunate.

In the late 16th century, the Jesuits were the lone missionaries operating in Japan. They had been placed under the protection of the king of Portugal and charged to pursue Portugal's national interest in Japan via missionary work in close collaboration with Portuguese sea trade.

Tokugawa Ieyasu, who ruled with hegemonic might, initially tried to regulate and oversee the silk trade with the Portuguese, but as the Jesuits were the ones in true control, he found this to be a difficult task.

Similarly, after Ieyasu used Spanish missionaries–such as Franciscans visiting from Manila–in his negotiations to begin commerce with Mexico, those same missionaries initiated missionary work at the behest of the king of Spain in Japan, leading to grave conflicts with the Jesuits. Ieyasu and the highest-ranking members of the shogunate understood that Christian theology lay at the heart of this equally matched turf war, and given that these two parties were ignoring the authority of the Japanese government, the shogunate began to think that Christianity itself had to be curbed to maintain social stability.

In 1612, a major bribery scandal between a powerful feudal lord and a close associate of Ieyasu came to light, resulting in the execution of both involved. As both individuals were also Christian, Christians were thereby proclaimed to be high-risk individuals and Christianity was officially outlawed soon after, kicking off the shogunate's suppression of the religion.

As mentioned before, Catholicism had spread furthest in Nagasaki, and in August of 1622, a total of 55 missionaries and followers were put to death by burning at the stake, crucifixion, or beheading.

In October of 1637, over 20,000 farmers in Shimabara, an area near Nagasaki, revolted against the oppressive policies of their feudal lord. Almost all of them were Christian and attacked in unison, leading to an order from the shogunate for a large number of feudal lords to muster forces for a subjugation army. The effort was a full-throated use of shogunate authority, eventually even leading to a mobilization of the Dutch presence. By the end of February of the following year, the rebellion had finally been quelled. The rebellion forces were nearly exterminated, but with great losses on the shogunate side as well.

Thereafter, the shogunate forbade all foreign trade, with the exception of China, some Asian countries and the Netherlands. This trade was limited to a single harbor in Nagasaki, subject to strict regulation and oversight. Furthermore, the coastal defenses of the entire country were strengthened and maintained in anticipation of a possible invasion, while the Dutch and Chinese presences were obligated to begin giving periodic reports on international affairs.

Meanwhile, to thoroughly stamp out Christianity domestically, the shogunate demanded all individuals to register as supporters of the existing Buddhist temples, while employing an anonymous neighbor reporting system to get tips on Christians in hiding. In spite of this, a large number of Christians held on to their Catholic faith, who resurfaced when the ban on Christianity was lifted.

In the midst of such social conditions, the Tokugawa shogunate also developed five highways (kaido) and side roads (wakaido) around Edo. In Kyushu, the Nagasaki Kaido - connecting Kokura and Nagasaki - was the only side road, with a total length of approximately 228 kilometers and 25 inns along the route. The Nagasaki Kaido played an important role as a 'road of civilization' that introduced Western culture and new technologies from Nagasaki, which was the only window for cultural exchange and trade with foreign countries such as the Netherlands and China under Japan's national isolation policies (sakoku). In addition to being used for visits to and from Edo by Nagasaki magistrates and the chief of the Dutch trading post, as well as the mandatory biannual commutes of feudal lords, the road was also frequently traveled by scholars and literary figures and used to traffic exotic animals such as elephants and peacocks. It was a busy route, indeed.

All foreign trade and exchange was limited to Dejima, the name of the off-shore trading post in Nagasaki that had been established for the Dutch. The Nagasaki Road was used to transport sugar from Dejima towards Kyoto, Osaka, and eventually Edo. As a result, foreign confectionery-making techniques were introduced along the route, and a number of famous confections were developed, leading to the emergence of a unique sugar culture known as the "Sugar Road."

The Nagasaki Road of yore is thus associated with a festive image of sweetness and peace.

In a bizarre coincidence, on August 9, 1995—the 50th anniversary of the atomic bombing of Nagasaki—I signed a contract to open an internal medicine clinic at a location along the old Nagasaki Road in Kinkeichou (golden rooster town) in Kokura. I knew nothing of the road's history at the time. Instead, my decision to open the clinic was triggered by my visit to the area to provide medical support after the Great Hanshin-Awaji Earthquake.

On January 17, 1995, as a young doctor working at a city hospital, I felt horribly restless after I heard the news about the disaster.

January 18 was a Wednesday. I was working at the Soka Gakkai's Kyushu headquarters, where I was engaged in the health management of staff every Wednesday afternoon, when I received information that a disaster relief headquarters had been set up by the Soka Gakkai to provide aid in the disaster area. Soka Gakkai is the Buddhist community that claims some five million members all throughout Japan, four hundred thousand in north America and offices in 192 countries overseas. As soon as I heard about this, I asked the staff of the Soka Gakkai's Kyushu headquarters to make arrangements for me to provide medical assistance.

For eight days, starting on January 20, I was involved in providing support to hundreds of nearby disaster victims who were housed at two Soka Gakkai facilities in Nishinomiya City and Higashinada Ward in Kobe City. It was then that I became keenly aware of just how important the role of "town doctor" becomes in such emergencies. In particular, when I was in Nishinomiya, a kind and gentlemanly doctor came to me with a house call bag in his hand and said, "I am a general practitioner in the neighborhood. Is there anything I can do for you? Is there anything you need?" I can't describe how wonderful I found this! Just him coming by to check in on me erased all of my exhaustion. I found him and what he was doing incredibly cool, and was left with a longing to become more like him.

So, on that sunny Wednesday afternoon of August 9, 1995, I was driving down a one-way street, aimlessly looking for a place to open my practice, when I saw a sign for a small real estate agency. I dropped in and asked, "I'd like to open an internal medicine clinic nearby; do you have any good properties available?" I quickly decided on one of the properties that they suggested. Looking back, it was a reckless way to start, and the trials and tribulations continued well after opening the clinic. Eight years passed, and when the business finally stabilized, I had that once-in-a-lifetime encounter with former Mayor Iccho Itoh. I did some research and discovered that my clinic was located along the Nagasaki Road. Next to our clinic is a pharmacy, through which that old highway apparently used to run. Our clinic is located about 10 km from Yahata, which was the last post station (shukuba) town along the route from Nagasaki to Kokura, and it is only 3.5 km from what was the highway's final stop, Muromachi. If Mr. Itoh had not told me about the Nagasaki Road, I likely never would have learned about this.

The coincidences kept stacking up. In the past, my clinic was connected to Nagasaki by a single road. I had decided to open my practice at this location on the 50th anniversary of the atomic bombing of Nagasaki. It all brought back to my mind the shock I felt when I stepped into the Atomic Bomb Museum back in the sixth grade of junior school. On that field trip, I felt a deep grief at the tragedy and cruelty of the bombing, and was stunned to learn that humanity still maintained enough of these weapons to destroy the Earth hundreds of times over. And to think that the bomb dropped on Nagasaki was originally intended for Kokura instead! There was a B-29 carrying an atomic bomb that made multiple flybys over Kokura on that day.

But how is that possible?

How did the presence of some clouds on a particular morning decide the fate of hundreds of thousands of people?

One day, when the sky was clear, I looked up at the sky over Kokura. I felt as if I could see a vision of the B-29 that was flying in the sky on August 9, 1945, carrying a nuclear weapon. To my surprise, I felt my eyes begin to fill with tears. This moment, this vision trapped me in such intense sadness that, for a time, I was unable to walk the streets of Kokura by myself.

Why are the people of Kokura so insensitive to this?

They might have been exposed to the atomic bomb themselves. How could they all remain so calm?

I spent a while in torment because of feelings such as these, but gradually, I too became engulfed again in the business of my daily life.

5. THE SHOOTING

April 17, 2007.

On this day, Nagasaki Mayor Iccho Itoh was campaigning for the upcoming mayoral election when he was shot twice from behind at close range in front of his campaign office by Japan Railroad Nagasaki Station. He had just gotten out of his car after an evening campaign stop when the attack occurred. The shooter was Tetsuya Shiroo, who was, at the time, the 59-year-old acting chairman of a designated crime syndicate (yakuza).

By the time the first report came in, Mr. Itoh appeared sure to succumb to his wounds. I desperately prayed for his resuscitation. However, he was confirmed dead at 2:28 a.m. on the following day, April 18th. I still remember the emptiness I felt at that time. Mayor Itoh was on track to be re-elected for a fourth term, but the shocking incident forced a restart in the mayoral election, and Mr. Tomihisa Taue, head of the Statistics Division of Nagasaki City Hall, won the election instead.

Mr. Itoh's predecessor, former Mayor Hitoshi Motoshima, had also been shot and seriously wounded. The perpetrator, a senior member of a right-wing group, was motivated by retaliation against Mayor Motoshima's suggestion that the Shōwa Emperor Hirohito bore responsibility for Japan's involvement in WWII. Of course, the attack was unforgivable, but questions of right or wrong aside, the motive was clear enough. After serving his 12-year sentence, this same person ran for mayor against Itoh, who was then running for a third term in office.

Tetsuya Shiroo's motive, on the other hand, poses more of a problem. Although Shiroo was apparently acquainted with the right-wing radical who shot Mr. Motoshima, he does not appear to have been involved in the shooting of Mr. Itoh. As the story goes, his long-standing conflicts with Nagasaki City Hall, including lingering resentment over his company being passed over for a Nagasaki loan funding program, was the motive for the attack on the mayor. However, he had no prior direct relationship with Mayor Itoh. Shiroo himself insisted during the trial that he had no particular desire to kill Itoh, and when asked why he killed the mayor, he stated, "Did I hate him? Why did I kill him? When you ask, no answer comes to mind".

Shiroo, who was sentenced to death in May 2008 and is now serving a life sentence after appeal, purportedly has said, "My reason for causing Mayor Itoh's death is an unending mystery to me." His criminal nature seems to be the product of a seriously disturbed mind. Meanwhile, the negative impact of Mayor Itoh's passing–the passing of a man who had been tireless in advocating for the abolition of nuclear weapons–seems very great indeed.

In Japan, where gun control is so widespread that only a very few Japanese people, such as police officers and hunters, are permitted to possess firearms, the shooting of a mayor is an extremely rare event. So why have there been two shootings of mayors in Nagasaki alone?

The only time I met Mr. Itoh, this all-too-human mayor, he loudly exclaimed to me, eyes wide in emphasis, "Man, we sure are lucky that a-bomb wasn't dropped on Kokura!" And yet, I miss him and grieve for him tremendously.

The mayor's death rekindled my thoughts once more about the nuclear attack on Nagasaki.

In between my medical appointments, I found myself again standing on land that was once the Nagasaki Road, looking up at the sky in contemplation.

What in the world was happening on August 9, 1945?

6. THE SUPERFORTRESS

The Mariana Islands, an archipelago of everlasting summer in the northwestern Pacific Ocean, is a paradise of white sand beaches, emerald green waters, endless blue skies, and star-filled night skies that attract many visitors.

Tinian Island is located 2,273 km southeast of Tokyo, 2,543 km from Hiroshima, 2,533 km from Nagasaki, and 9,759 km west of San Diego. At the beginning of World War II, it was a military base occupied by the Japanese Army. However, by the Battle of Tinian (July 24–August 2, 1944), it was under the occupation of the U.S. Army. During the battle, 8,010 of the 8,500 Japanese troops involved were killed in action, compared to 328 of the 54,000 American troops involved.

The island of Guam was recaptured by the U.S. in the roughly concurrent Battle of Guam (July 21 to August 10, 1944), in which 18,500 of 22,500 Japanese troops and 2,124 out of 55,000 U.S. troops were killed.

The Battle of Saipan was fought from June 15 to July 9, 1944, during which time, 25,000 of the 32,000-strong Japanese army were killed and another 5,000 committed "self-determination" (jiketsu; suicide). The U.S. forces, numbering 127,000, emerged victorious, with 3,551 killed or missing in action. Japanese civilian deaths at Saipan numbered more than 10,000, and many civilians were killed on other islands as well.

Following these battles, a great number of B-29s, which are considered in aviation history to be "the greatest aircraft of the 20th century," were flown to military bases that were built on Tinian, Guam, and Saipan to carry out strategic bombing raids on the Japanese mainland. The B-29 was 30 meters long and 43 meters wide. It was called 'the plane from the future' because of its handsome, shiny and silver body and outstanding performance by the standards of the time. It had a range of over 5,000 kilometers—twice that of a conventional heavy bomber. It flew at an altitude of 10,000 meters, far above the practical altitude of 5,000 to 7,000 meters of its contemporaries. At this altitude, even enemy high-performance fighters could not compete properly due to reduced mobility, and most flak could not reach this altitude either.

In other words, it was a "dream plane" that could bomb freely without fear of enemy counterattack.

The total development cost for the plane was $3 billion, 1.5 times the cost of the Manhattan Project that had developed the atomic bomb.

Truk Island, known as "Japan's Pearl Harbor," had already fallen into the hands of the U.S. military by this point, and in the battle between Japan and the U.S. over the Philippines, the Battle of Leyte Gulf in October of 1944 the Imperial Japanese Navy suffered a crushing defeat that effectively ended Japan's naval power in the Pacific theater.

Thus, by this point, the Philippines had been recaptured by the U.S., Japan had suffered a number of humiliating losses, and the U.S. was buoyed by a string of decisive victories. It was under these circumstances that the indiscriminate incendiary bombardments of residential areas in Tokyo and other Japanese cities were launched, one after another, from the Mariana Islands. In less than a year, most major Japanese cities had been burned to the ground, claiming 460,000 lives.

At first, when a B-29 formation approached a Japanese city, an air raid alarm would be sounded, anti-aircraft guns opened fire, and fighter planes took off to intercept. Some of the fighters, unable to take out the B-29s by firefight, took them down through deliberate mid-air crashes instead. Over time, however, the capacity to resist the B-29s was completely lost, and cities became helpless against the firebombing. Urban-dwelling Japanese began to pay little attention if they saw a few B-29s flying overhead, hoping that they were simply engaged in reconnaissance or weather observation.

7. HOW WAS THE NAGASAKI BOMBING REPORTED?

On August 31, 1946, The *New Yorker* magazine devoted its entire issue to John Hersey's "HIROSHIMA," in which he reported to Americans and the world the full, ghastly realities of atomic warfare in that city, featuring testimonies from six of the only humans in history to survive nuclear attack. The following is a quote from the book (modified by the author) regarding Dr. Sasaki.

> *Dr. Terufumi Sasaki, a Red Cross Hospital surgeon, was on a train on the way to the hospital. At the terminus, he caught a streetcar at once. (He later calculated that if he had taken his customary train that morning, and if he had had to wait a few minutes for the streetcar, as often happened, he would have been close to the center at the time of explosion and would surely have perished.) He arrived at the hospital at seven-forty and reported to the chief surgeon. A few minutes later, he went to a room on the first floor and drew blood from the arm of a man in order to perform a Wassermann test. The laboratory containing the incubators for the test was on the third floor. With the blood specimen in his left hand, walking in a kind of distraction he had felt all morning, probably because of the dream and his restless night, he started along the main corridor on his way toward the stairs. He was one step beyond an open window when the light of the bomb was reflected, like a gigantic photographic flash, in the corridor. He ducked down on one knee. Just then, the blast ripped through the hospital. The glasses he was wearing*

flew off his face; the bottle of blood crashed against one wall; his Japanese slippers zipped out from under his feet.

The hospital was in horrible confusion: heavy partitions and ceilings had fallen on patients, beds had overturned, windows had blown in and cut people, blood was spattered on the walls and floors, instruments were everywhere, many of the patients were running about screaming, many more lay dead. Dr. Sasaki's patient, whom he had just left and who a few moments before had been dreadfully afraid of syphilis, was also dead. Dr Sasaki found himself the only doctor in the hospital who was unhurt.

Dr. Sasaki, who believed that the enemy had hit only the building he was in, got bandages and began to bind the wounds of those inside the hospital; while outside, all over Hiroshima, maimed and dying citizens turned their unsteady steps toward the Red Cross Hospital to begin an invasion...

Until Hersey's story appeared in the New Yorker, the U.S. government had astonishingly managed to hide the magnitude of what happened in Hiroshima immediately after the bombing, and successfully covered up the bomb's long-term deadly radiological effects. U.S. officials in Washington D.C., and occupation officials in Japan suppressed, contained, and spun reports from the ground in Hiroshima and Nagasaki until the story all but disappeared from the headlines and the public's consciousness.

Times have changed an in November 1980, a movie about the nuclear attack on Hiroshima was released. The title was 'Enola Gay: The Men, the Mission, the Atomic Bomb' which was *a carefully documented history lesson showing the decision to drop the atomic bomb on Hiroshima, the secrecy surrounding the training of the men, and finally the flight of the Enola Gay on August 6, 1945* (Pittsburg Post-Gazette). However, the film does not depict any of the tragic scenes of the remaining corpses and writhing wounded in Hiroshima after the bombing. Now, here are quite a lot of reports that have been published on the Hiroshima disaster.

At midnight on August 6, a three-plane formation launched a sortie from Tinian. The nuclear bomb was carried by the Enola Gay, accompanied by The Great Artiste and Dimples 91. The three aircraft returned to Tinian Island after the nuclear attack on Hiroshima.

As far as I have been able to determine, it is not known exactly when construction of the gun-barrel-type nuclear weapon that was dropped on Hiroshima (Little Boy) was completed. In comparison, the first confirmed success of the other model, an implosion-type nuclear weapon, is well-known: it was successfully detonated on July 16, 1945, in the Trinity test. It was one of these models, "Fat Man," that was dropped on Nagasaki.

On the other hand, as far as I have been able to find, there is no film or other film that systematically describes the nuclear bombing of Nagasaki in as much detail as 'Enola Gay' does.

I'll now present all that I have been able to find on reports detailing the nuclear attack on Nagasaki. This book may be the first attempt to bring together all such information in this way. Therefore, although these quotations are lengthy, I present them below in chronological order of publication, in the hope that a comparative study of their contents will help in revealing the truth.

7. 1 THE NEW YORK TIMES, AUG. 9, 1945

First, let's look at an article from The New York Times published immediately after the attack. It reads as follows:

> *SOVIET DECLARES WAR ON JAPAN; ATTACKS MANCHURIA, TOKYO SAYS; ATOM BOMB LOOSED ON NAGASAKI*
>
> *2d Big Aerial Blow*
> *Japanese Port is Target in Devastating New Midday Assault*

Result Called Good

For Asserts Hiroshima Toll Is `Uncountable`--Assails `Atrocity`

By W. H. LAWRENCE

Guam, Thursday, Aug.9—Gen. Carl A. Spaatz announced today that a second atomic bomb had been dropped, this time on the city of Nagasaki, and that crew members reported "good results."

The second use of the new and terrifying secret weapon which wiped out more than 60 percent of the city of Hiroshima and, according to the Japanese radio, killed every resident of that town, occurred at noon today, Japanese time. The target today was an important industrial and shipping area with a population of about 258,000.

The great bomb, which harnesses the power of the universe to destroy the enemy by concussion, blast and fire, was dropped on the second enemy city about seven hours after the Japanese had received a political "roundhouse punch" in the form of a declaration of war by the Soviet Union.

Vital Transshipment Point

Guam, Thursday, Aug. 9 (AP)—

Nagasaki is vitally important as a port for transshipment of military supplies and the embarkation of troops in support of Japan's operations in China, Formosa, Southeast Asia, and the Southwest Pacific. It was highly important as a major shipbuilding and repair center for both naval and merchantmen.

The city also included industrial suburbs of Inase and Akunoura on the western side of the harbor, and Urakami. The combined area is nearly double Hiroshima's.

Nagasaki, although only two-thirds as large as Hiroshima in population, is considered more important industrially. With a population now estimated at 258,000, its twelve square miles are jap-packed with the eave-to-eave buildings that on it the name of "sea of roofs."

General Spaatz's communique reporting the bombing did not say whether one or more than one "mighty atom" was dropped.

As far as I can tell from reading this article, there is no mention of multiple targets for the bombing. The logical conclusion is that Nagasaki was attacked simply because it was an important area from a munition's standpoint. Of course, in reality, the bombs detonated over the residential area of Urakami, causing only minor damage to munitions factories and killing or wounding an unspeakable number of civilians.

7. 2 FROM THE REPORT WRITTEN BY THE 1946 PULITZER PRIZE WINNER

On September 9th, 1945, The New York Times published an article by William Leonard Laurence headlined "WINNING WORK—Atomic Bombing of Nagasaki Told By Flight Member," which detailed his eyewitness account of the atomic bombing of Nagasaki. The following excerpts maintain the thematic consistency of this book. For his ten articles on the development, production, and significance of the atomic bomb, including this article, W. L. Laurence became the recipient of the 1946 Pulitzer Prize in Reporting. He is a different person to 'William H. Lawrence' who was a political reporter at The New York Times.

The quotation is a bit long, but it is a detailed record of the immediate aftermath of the nuclear attack on Nagasaki. When this report is contrasted with the reports of others, including reports given by crew members much later in their lives, a number of problems emerge.

WITH THE ATOMIC BOMB MISSION TO JAPAN

Aug.9 (Delayed)-We are on our way to bomb the mainland of Japan. Our flying contingent consists of three specially designed B-29 "Superforts," and two of these carry no bombs. But our lead plane is on its way with another atomic bomb, the second in three days, concentrating in its active substance an explosive energy equivalent to 20,000 and, under favorable conditions, 40,000 tons of TNT.

We have several chosen targets. One of these is the great industrial and shipping center of Nagasaki, on the western shore of Kyushu, one of the main islands of the Japanese homeland.

The briefing at midnight revealed the extreme care and the tremendous amount of preparation that had been made to take care of every detail of the mission, to make certain that the atomic bomb fully served the purpose for which it was intended. Each target in turn was shown in detailed maps and aerial photographs. Every detail of the course was rehearsed—navigation, altitude, weather, where to land in emergencies…

In command of our mission is Maj. Charles W. Seeney (Sweeny in correct, author), 25. His flagship, carrying the atomic bomb; is named The Great Artiste, but the name does not appear on the body of the great silver ship, with its unusually long, four-bladed, orange-tipped propellers. Instead it carried the number 77, and someone remarks that that it was "Red" Grange's winning number on the gridiron.

Major S(w)eeney's co-pilot is First Lieut. Charles D. Albury. The bombardier, upon whose shoulders rests the responsibility of depositing the atomic bomb square on its target, is Capt. Kermit K. Beahan who is celebrating his twenty-seventh birthday today.

The navigator on The Great Artiste is Capt. James F. Van Pelt Jr. The flight engineer is M/Sgt. John D. Kuharek. Albert T. De Hart is the tail gunner; the radar operator is S/Sgt. Edward K. Buckley. The radio operator is Sgt. Abe M. Spitzer. Sgt. Raymond Gallagher is assistant flight engineer.

The lead ship is also carrying a group of scientific personnel, headed by Comdr. Frederick L. Ashworth, USN, one of the leaders in the development of the bomb. The group includes Lieut. Jacob Beser, an expert on airborne radar.

The other two Superfortresses in our formation are instrument planes, carrying special apparatus to measure the power of the bomb at the time of explosion, high speed cameras and other photographic equipment.

Our "Superfort"is the second in line. Its commander is Capt. Frederick C. Bock. Its other officers are Second Lieut. Hugh C. Fergson, pilot; Second Lieut. Leonard A. Godfrey, navigator; and First Lieut. Charles Levy, bombardier.

The enlisted personnel of this "Superfort" are: T/Sgt. Roderick F. Arnold, flight engineer; Sgt. Ralph D. Curry, radio operator; Sgt. William 6. Barney, radar operator; Corp. Robert J. Stock, assistant flight engineer, and Corp. Ralph D. Belanger, tail gunner.

The scientific personnel of our "Superfort" include S/Sgt. Walter Goodman and Lawrence Johnson, a graduate student at the University of California.

The third "Superfort" is commanded by Maj. James Hopkins. His officers are Second Lieut. John E. Caution, pilot; Second Lieut. Stanley C. Steinke, navigator; and Second Lieut. Myron Faryna, bombardier.
On this "Superfort" are also two distinguished from Britain, whose scientists played an important role in the development of the atomic bomb.

We took off at 2:50 this morning and headed northwest on a straight line for the Empire.

We were about an hour away from our base when the storm broke. Our great ship took some heavy dips through the abysmal darkness around us but it took these dips much more gracefully than a large commercial airliner.

By 4:50 it was real light outside. We had lost our lead ship, but Lieutenant Godfrey, our navigator, informs me that we had arranged for that contingency. We have an assembly point in the sky above the little island of Yakoshima, southeast of Kyushu, at 9:10. We are to circle there and wait for the rest of our formation.

Our weather planes ahead of us are on their way to find out where the wind blows.

Captain Bock informs me that we are about to start our climb to bombing altitude.

He manipulates a few knobs on his control panel to the right of him and I alternately watch the white clouds and ocean below me and the altimeter on the bombardier's panel. We reached our altitude at 8 o'clock. We were then over Japanese waters, close to their mainland. Lieutenant Godfrey motioned to me to look through his radar scope. Before me was the outline of our assembly point. We shall soon meet our lead ship and proceed to the final stage of our journey.

We reached Yakoshima at 8:12 and there, about 4,000 feet ahead of us, was The Great Artiste with its precious load. I saw Lieutenant Godfrey and Sergeant Curry strap on their parachutes and I decided to do likewise. We started circling. We saw little towns on the coastline, heedless of our presence. We kept on circling, waiting for the third ship in our formation.

It was 8:56 when we began heading for the coastline. Our weather scouts had sent us code messages, deciphered by Sergeant Curry, informing us that both the primary target as well as the secondary were clearly visible.

The winds of destiny seemed to favor certain Japanese cities that must remain nameless. We circled about them again and again and found no opening in the thick umbrella of clouds that covered them. Destiny chose Nagasaki as the ultimate target.

We had been circling for some time when we noticed black puffs of smoke coming through the white clouds directly at us. There were fifteen bursts of flak in rapid succession, all too low. Captain Bock changed his course. There soon followed eight more bursts of flak, right up to our altitude, but by this time were too far to the left.

We flew southward down the channel and at 10:33 crossed the coastline and headed straight for Nagasaki about 100 miles to the west. Here again we circled until we found an opening in the clouds. It was 11:01 and the goal of our mission had arrived.

We heard the prearranged signal on our radio, put on our arc-welder's glasses and watched tensely the maneuvering of the strike ship about half a mile in front of us.

"There she goes!" someone said.

Out of the belly of The Great Artiste what looked like a black object went downward.

Captain Bock swung around to get out of range; but even though we were turning away in the opposite direction, and despite the fact that it was broad daylight in our cabin, all of us became aware of a giant flash that broke through the dark barrier of our arc-welder's lenses and flooded our cabin with intense light.

Then, just when it appeared as though the thing has settled down into a state of permanence, there came shooting out of the top a giant mushroom that increased the height of the pillar to a total of 45,000 feet. The mushroom top was even more alive than the pillar, seething and boiling in a white fury of creamy foam, sizzling upward and then descending earthward, a thousand Old Faithful geysers rolled into one.

As the first mushroom floated off into the blue it changed its shape into a, flowerlike form, its giant petal curving downward, creamy white outside, rose-colored inside. It still retained that shape when we last gazed at it from a distance of about 200 miles.

Note: The above are a series of excerpts from the article "WINNING WORK—Atomic Bombing of Nagasaki Told By Flight Member." While I have selected these excerpts for their immediate relevance to this book, the text itself is the same as the original, except for the correction of "Seeny" to "Sweeney" and the time being corrected to Japan Standard Time. The original can be easily obtained from the Pulitzer Prizes website.

Reading W. L. Laurence's report in its entirety, I feel that although it was written within a year of the nuclear bombings, it is somewhat vague and lacking in specifics. Most notably, the six letters of 'Kokura' do not appear anywhere in his report. The name of the place, which must have been extremely important as the primary target for the nuclear bombing squadron, is not even traced in his detailed military report, which was written only a year after the bombing. And, as readers will notice, there is not even a trace of it in the detailed military report, which was written only a year after the bombing. By comparison, the report that follows, written by Commander Ashworth of the Navy and Major Sweeney of the Army almost half a century after the bombings, is as realistic as watching a movie.

W. L. Laurence published a number of works in later years, such as "Dawn Over Zero", and "The Hell Bomb", that detail nuclear weapons in a positive light.

By the way, I learned of the existence of this article from "'FALLOUT'—The Hiroshima Cover-up and the Reporter Who Revealed It to the World" by Lesley M. M. Blume, published in August 2020. This book is full of content that supports the claims made in 'Revive The Bells of Nagasaki!' which

I published in Japan in April 2019. As an amateur, I only have a limited amount of time to write, so, it is very heartening to know that a professional writer like Lesley Blume is working on this kind of work.

7. 3 SPEECH OF THE MAYOR OF KOKURA 1946

In the fall of 1946, the mayor of Kokura made an appeal to the citizens of the city titled "Proclamation to Our 150,000 Citizens in Recognition of August 9." I happened upon it in the recently opened Kitakyushu Peace Museum. The following is a quotation of the text, which I first partially translated into modern Japanese to facilitate English translation.

> *August 9, Showa 20 (1945). On this day, a thick miasma hung in the overcast sky.*
>
> *The power and devastation of the atomic bomb in Hiroshima sent 150,000 citizens into a state of terror.*
>
> *"I hear Kokura is next."*
>
> *Rumors such as these sprang from nowhere, spreading everywhere. Alarms were issued constantly, and a flurry of defensive measures and evacuations were issued throughout the night and day, in the midst of heat and starvation.*
>
> *Such heat! Like phantoms, a number of B-29s swooped down over Kokura, penetrating the thick air, towards Mt. Hobashira.*
>
> *This was a life-or-death moment for the people of Kitakyushu, and especially the 150,000 residents of Kokura. A few minutes later, a second atomic bomb, the weapon that had fundamentally transformed what it means to be human just days before, unleashed a hellscape of unparalleled horror and acidity on the port city of Nagasaki.*
>
> *The old port city of Nagasaki! In one terrifying moment, Nagasaki, the*

heroic city of West Kyushu, had its dreams for the future, its beautiful past full of bright traditions, all but destroyed, along with hundreds of thousands of human sacrifices.

A recent report in a newspaper tells us that, "The plan was to drop the bomb on Kokura, but due to weather conditions, the target was quickly changed to Nagasaki."

Even now, our blood curdles at the memory of what had transpired.

Kokura, permitted to live on!

Nagasaki, poor Nagasaki!

On this anniversary of defeat, let us once again make comparison. Even while the line between fortune and misfortune may be paper-thin, is not this difference between Kokura, which has never known war damage, and Nagasaki, which will be forever remembered in world history for the devastation it suffered, altogether too great?

On this day, let us express our deep, sincere grief for the citizens of Nagasaki who took our place, and let us show our enthusiasm for helping Nagasaki rebuild. Let us do so with compassion and a spirit of mutual assistance towards our neighbors, and let us help foster a sense of renewal in this desolate and ruined city, as pioneers in the reconstruction of our country.

We offer our heartfelt condolences to the victims of the disaster that befell Nagasaki at 11:00 a.m. on August 9, the moment of the nuclear explosion, and offer our prayers for all the people of Nagasaki as we reflect on this tragedy.

In closing, the City of Nagasaki has contacted us regarding the relief fund for its citizens. To ensure our rapid response, it will be most efficient for each neighborhood section of City Hall to collect donations locally and request that they be sent to the City of Nagasaki.

September 8, 1946

Ryosuke Hamada, Mayor of Kokura City

This appeal by the mayor of Kokura was no doubt subjected to strict oversight by GHQ (the Occupation Forces), who exercised intense information control. When compared to the content of the interviews I will present later in this book from citizens who remember the situation in Kokura as it actually was on August 9, 1945, the content of this statement is quite incongruous. In particular, the statement that a nuclear explosion occurred in Nagasaki a few minutes after the shadow of a number of B-29s emerged from Kokura to Mt. Hobashira is something that even modern supersonic fighter planes would not be able to do, given the distance between Kokura and Nagasaki. Perhaps the US military wanted to defend themselves against the worldwide condemnation of the nuclear bombing of Nagasaki, a holy Catholic city, by saying that the bombing of Nagasaki was done out of force majeure.

In addition, the mayor said, "Kokura, permitted to live on! Nagasaki, poor Nagasaki!"

I wonder how the citizens of Kokura must have felt when they were told that they could have been exposed to the atomic bombing of Nagasaki. As the devastation of Nagasaki was reported, they must have keenly felt how lucky they were. They must have come to believe that it was the U.S. that had brought them such luck, and this must have increased the momentum to cooperate with the U.S. military in the Cold War between the U.S. and the Soviet Union that led to the outbreak of the Korean War.

7.4 DR. NAGAI'S "THE BELLS OF NAGASAKI" 1949

Next, let's look at a related excerpt from the novel "The Bells of Nagasaki" written by Dr. Takashi Nagai, which was published in 1949 after being censored by GHQ (the Occupation Forces). "The Bells of Nagasaki" is a non-fiction account that begins a few days before the second atomic bombing on August 9, 1945 and continues until Christmas, 1945. The author, a devout

Catholic, was a 37-year-old radiologist at Nagasaki Medical College Hospital at the time, which was located about 500 meters from Ground Zero.

Dr. Nagai wrote;

On August 9, 1945, at 10:30 A.M. a meeting of the Supreme Council of War was held at the Imperial Headquarters to decide whether Japan should capitulate or continue to wage war. At that moment the world was at a crossroads. A decision was being made that would either bring about a new and lasting peace or throw the human family into further cruel bloodshed and carnage.

And just at that same time, at two minutes past eleven in the morning, an atomic bomb exploded over our district of Urakami in Nagasaki. In an instant, eight thousand Christians were called into the hands of God, while in a few hours the fierce flames reduced to ashes this sacred territory of the East. At midnight of that same night the cathedral suddenly burst into flames and was burned to the ground. And exactly at that time in the Imperial Palace, His Majesty the Emperor made known his sacred decision to bring the war to an end.

On August 15, the Imperial Rescript which put an end to the fighting was formally promulgated, and the whole world welcomed a day of peace. This day was also the great feast of the Assumption of the Virgin Mary. It is significant to reflect that Urakami Cathedral was dedicated to her. And we must ask if this convergence of events—the ending of the war and the celebration of her feast—was merely coincidental or if there was here some mysterious providence of God.

I have heard that the second atomic bomb, calculated to deal a deadly blow to the war potential of Japan, was originally destined for another city. But since the sky over that city was covered with clouds, the American pilots found it impossible to aim at their target. Consequently, they suddenly changed their plans and decided to drop the bomb on Nagasaki, the second-

ary target. However, yet another hitch occurred. As the bomb fell, cloud and wind carried it slightly north of the munitions factories over which it was supposed to explode, and it exploded above the cathedral.

This is what I have heard. If it is true, the American pilots did not aim at Urakami. It was the providence of God that carried the bomb to that destination.

Is there not a profound relationship between the destruction of Urakami and the end of the war? Urakami, the only holy place in all Japan—was it not chosen as a victim, a pure lamb, to be slaughtered and burned on the altar of sacrifice to expiate the sins committed by humanity in the Second World War?

The human family has inherited the sin of Adam who ate the fruit of the forbidden tree; we have inherited the sin of Cain who killed his younger brother; we have forgotten that we are children of God; we have believed in idols; we have disobeyed that law of love. Joyfully we have hated one another; joyfully we have killed one another. And now at last we have brought this world it was not sufficient to repent. We had to obtain God's pardon through the offering of a great sacrifice.

While Dr. Nagai suffered from leukemia and was a survivor of the bombing himself, he was devoted to his work as a radiologist at a university hospital, offering community healthcare for ordinary people. After the bombing, he continued to provide medical support to survivors, but his own ailments led to severe bleeding and critical illness at one point. After undergoing censorship by the Occupation, his writings were published in 1949.

Dr. Nagai wrote, *If it is true, the American pilots did not aim at Urakami. It was the providence of God that carried the bomb to that destination.*

However, in this book I concluded, it was not true . Dr. Nagai's story will be discussed in greater detail later in the book.

7. 5 FROM THE TEXTBOOK FOR STUDENTS IN JAPAN 1962

One of Japan's leading companies Shueisha published a textbook for elementary and junior high school students titled "Junior Edition: History of the Pacific War, Volume 4." The company used the best writers in Japan at that time for this project. The section that described the nuclear attack on Hiroshima contained the following statement:

> *The horror that befell the civilians of Hiroshima was of a hellish, grotesque intensity unmatched by any battlefield.*
>
> *Nonetheless, the US dropped a second atomic bomb, this time on Nagasaki, on August 9.*
>
> *This second atomic bomb was of different construction compared to the one that was dropped on Hiroshima.*
>
> *For the mission, one Major Sweeney was appointed as commander, with Lieutenant Alburi as his co-pilot. The sighting officer was Captain Beehan, the flight officer was Captain James, and the plane that carried the bomb was named The Great Artiste.*
>
> *What is "artistic" about a weapon meant to end human lives?*
>
> *As in the case of Hiroshima, the plane departed from Tinian at 3:50 a.m. on the 9th, in a formation of three planes. This time, however, the other two planes were occupied by nuclear physicists and Royal Air Force pilots, as well as machines for measuring explosive power, ultra-high-speed cameras, and photographic equipment.*
>
> *The first target was Nagasaki, the second Kokura. The weather monitors that had flown in an hour earlier reported good weather and not too many clouds in either of the two cities.*
>
> *The Great Artiste chose Nagasaki. However, looking under the wings, the clouds over Nagasaki were so thick that it was difficult to attack the city with the naked eye.*

The pilots had been ordered not to use radar for the atomic bombing, but rather to bomb the target with the naked eye.

Therefore, they considered flying towards Kokura, the second target, but it would have taken quite a while before they could get weather confirmation on Kokura conditions. They feared that even if they went to Kokura, they would be met by clouds again.

(Let's wait for the clouds to clear.)

Such was Major Sweeney's deliberation. The Great Artiste continued to circle around and around, above the clouds over Nagasaki.

Beneath the clouds were people who merely wanted peace. The Nagasaki Medical College Hospital, located on a hill next to the brick cathedral in Urakami, was staffed by Dr. Takashi Nagai, a Catholic professor at the Nagasaki Medical College (Dr. Nagai later wrote a book about his experience of the atomic bombing, "The Bells of Nagasaki").

The plane circled for two hours over Nagasaki and western Kyushu.

At 12:01 a.m. (11:01 a.m. Japan time), the Great Artiste finally spotted a break in the clouds over Nagasaki.

The atomic bomb was dropped.

A huge atomic cloud, different from the one over Hiroshima, billowed up to a height of 14,000 meters.

The explosion killed 36,000 people, left 40,000 injured, and destroyed all buildings in a 4.662-kilometer, or roughly 3-mile, radius. In the days, months, and years to come, many more victims would emerge in the form of "A-Bomb Disease": radiation poisoning.

The Great Artiste, after circling repeatedly over Nagasaki, had ran out of gasoline and was unable to return to Tinian, landing in Okinawa instead.

Thus, were the victims of the atomic bombs confirmed: Hiroshima. Nagasaki.

In 1962, Shueisha was (and still remains) one of Japan's leading publishers; this textbook was likely present in elementary and junior high school libraries throughout Japan. By that time, publication was no longer subject to GHQ (Occupation) censorship. While a book such as this, given its influence on the public, would have been subject to oversight from authorities in both Japan and the United States, note that the authors of this book were Yoshiro Akinaga and Hiroshi Muneta: both first-rate writers. These writers clearly state that "Nagasaki was the primary target." It is unclear what references they uncovered to justify their position here. However, given their reputation, it seems likely that they would have made such a claim based on some sort of compelling evidence.

In 1954, the United States conducted a hydrogen bomb test at the Bikini Atoll. The captain of the Daigo Fukuryū Maru, a Japanese far-seas tuna fishing vessel, was exposed to a large amount of nuclear fallout (shi no hai, or 'ashes of death') and died of radiation poisoning. This incident triggered an anti-nuclear-weapons movement throughout all of Japan. In response, the authorities in Japan and the United States took various measures to suppress the anti-nuclear movement; by the time of the publication of this textbook, the situation in Japan had somewhat calmed down. Notably, the Cuban Missile Crisis of October 1962 had forced the United States into a position where it lacked the diplomatic leeway to strongly influence publications of this nature in Japan, which likely also factored into its final contents, given the timing of its publication.

7. 6 "THE POSTMAN OF NAGASAKI" BY PETER TOWNSEND 1984

Townsend was a professional airman who proved himself as a brilliant fighter pilot in the Battle of Britain. After the war, he became a writer and traveled the world to write books about wartime child victims. "The Postman of Nagasaki" tells the story of Sumiteru Taniguchi, who was exposed to radiation while delivering mail and miraculously survived the bombing. In it, he describes the scene of the nuclear bombing of Nagasaki. The following is a quote from that book.

> *The Japanese inner cabinet, the Big Six, had been summoned to an emergency meeting on the morning of 9 August, to hear (Prime Minister) Suzuki announce his intention of accepting unconditional surrender. It was 11 a.m. At that very moment, Sweeney's B.29, having been thwarted by clouds over Kokura, was starting its bombing run on the secondary target, Nagasaki.*
>
> *The aircraft, named Bock's Car after Captain Frederick Bock Jr. who usually flew it, had taken off from Tinian just before 4 a.m. (3 a.m. Japanese time). Hardly had it settled on course than there was trouble with the fuel circuit, but Sweeney pressed on north towards the primary target, Kokura. He found the city obscured by smoke and haze. Bombardier Kermit Beahan had orders to make a visual drop, but on each of the aircraft's three runs over the city he had to report to the captain on the intercom: 'I can't pick up the aiming point.' Those few, frustrated words meant that Kokura was spared, Nagasaki condemned. Badly worried by the fuel shortage charge of the bomb—'I can only make one run.' If the aiming point could not be identified visually, Ashworth had orders to jettison the bomb over the sea. What was a waste, he thought. The 200,000 people below in Nagasaki would have disagreed, but it was the young naval commander alone who at this moment held power of life and death over them. He decided to disobey orders. Nagasaki was on the radar-scope. 'Go ahead then and bomb by radar,' he shouted to Sweeney.*
>
> *It was 11 a.m. local time, Beahan, peering down, suddenly cried out, 'I can see the city.' But he could only see part of it; the down-town area where the aiming point lay was hidden by cloud. Beahan had his sights*

on an oval stadium; it was the Ohashi stadium where Sumiteru had once been chased by the blacksmith's dogs, on the left bank of the Urakami river, three kilometers up the valley from the intended aiming point. 'It will have to do,' the bombardier decided. The bomb would devastate the whole of Nagasaki, anyway. He pressed the release and Sweeny, to escape the blast, banked Bock's Car into a dive away from the city. The bomb fell free for about forty seconds; the burst-point ('epicentre') had been pre-set at a height of some five hundred meters above ground level. The maximum force of the explosion was concentrated at a point on the ground directly below (the 'hypocentre'). It was two hundred meters away from Beahan's aiming point and in the heart of Urakami district. No district in Nagasaki could have answered better to the target definition. With its private houses, its schools and hospitals, its university, temples and cathedral, its parks and peaceful tree-lined streets, Urakami district was the very model of an urban area. Out of its midst, there burst a giant ball of fire, hotter than the sun, belching smoke, and towering skywards for five kilometers in a dense orange-black column from the top of which there issued a heaving mass of cloud, mushroom-shaped and seething with radioactive dust and vapor. Somewhere at the foot of that column lay Sumiteru.

Although similar in content to the reports of those responsible for the execution of the nuclear bombing squads, the following statements should be noted.

Beahan had his sights on an oval stadium; it was the Ohashi stadium where Sumiteru had once been chased by the blacksmith's dogs, on the left bank of the Urakami river, three kilometers up the valley from the intended aiming point.

It was two hundred meters away from Beahan's aiming point and in the heart of Urakami district. No district in Nagasaki could have answered better to the target definition.

Peter Townsend, in his experience as a former military officer, makes a meaningful reference to the nuclear bombing sites. As we will be discussing this point in the future, I would like you to memorize the contents of this text.

Peter Townsend was a brave fighter pilot with many battle records. In other words, he took the lives of many enemy soldiers as an act of wartime combat. However, as you can see from the trajectory of his life after his mission as a fighter pilot, he was essentially a gentleman knight who respected compassion for the weak and defenseless. He and Princess Margaret, Countess of Snowdon, fell in love. For various reasons, Mr. Townsend eventually married another woman, and the story became the subject of the movie "Roman Holiday." I am sure that Mr. Townsend was an excellent pilot under orders from the top.

If the top brass had ordered him to be a good pilot and assigned to the nuclear bombing squadron, he would have refused, even at the risk of his own life.

His daughter Isabelle Townsend became a Ralph Lauren model in the late 1980s and early 1990s. She told me she was looking forward to reading the book when I offered to present it to her upon its publication during her visit to Kokura, Japan, in the summer of 2022.

7.7 ASHWORTH 1987

In September 1987, former Navy Lieutenant General Frederick L. Ashworth contributed a long-form report to "Shipmate" titled "The Second Atomic Bombing: Nagasaki." This submission occurred 42 years after the bombing, when Ashworth was 75 years old. He was a Lieutenant Commander in the Navy at the time of the Nagasaki nuclear attack, and had the authority of

"Weaponer" or "Bomb Commander" on board the plane carrying the atomic bomb. Although he was ordered to drop the atomic bomb on Nagasaki visually, he received further authorization as well, as follows:

> *A further important restriction of the tactical procedures for the operations was a directive from Washington that in case the delivery aircraft should reach the target and find visual bombing impossible, it should return to base with the bomb. The drop should be made with radar only if the plane could not otherwise return. The latter provision was an important consideration in one of the most important decisions made by the Weaponer in the attack on Nagasaki.*

In contrast to W. L. Laurence's September 1945 Pulitzer Prize Report WINNING WORK, which said that The Great Artiste was the aircraft carrying the atomic bomb in the sortie on August 9, 1945, Ashworth wrote the following:

> *Take off for the launch of the Nagasaki mission was scheduled for 0345 on August 9th. Capt. Bock's aircraft named BOCK'S CAR had been selected as the bomb-carrying plane since Maj. Sweeney's plane, the GREAT ARTISTE, named after Maj. Beahan the bombardier in his crew, had mechanical troubles which precluded its use.*

The following quotes from the text of the report show how the pilots approached the bombing target. Three planes were scheduled to meet over Yakushima (written as "Ykashima"), but after failing to confirm sighting of one of the planes, the other two planes headed for Kokura, the first target, and then switched their focus to Nagasaki, the second target.

> *It was decided that we continue our flight to Kokura as planned, climbing to the bombing altitude of 30,000 feet, with the hope that our companion*

B-29 was the one we wanted.

During our approach to Kokura, Lt. Barnes again ran a check of the bomb components and found everything normal. The aircraft was under the control of the bombardier as he manipulated his Mark XV Norden bomb sight. The meteorological conditions did not look very favorable, not because of weather phenomenon in the area, but because of a dense haze. The bombardier found that it was impossible to positively identify the target. It became even more frustrating when, as the aircraft reached a position nearly directly over the target it became visible, but by then there was not sufficient time for him to synchronize his bomb sight to permit release of the bomb. This is a common situation when haze if present; the atmosphere is more or less opaque when viewed from a distance as was the case of our slant range to the target, and then, as less of the contaminated air is needed to be penetrated while viewing from directly above, it becomes possible to see the ground clearly. We attributed the dense haze to the fact that a neighboring city had been attacked with incendiary bombs the previous night and the resulting smoke was aggravating the haze condition. Under these circumstances it was not possible to attack the target visually as our instructions required.

It occurred to me that there might be a possibility of having better visibility if the bombing approach was made from a different direction. Therefore, I directed Maj. Sweeny to maneuver in such a way as to make a second bombing run on a course 120 degrees from that of the initial approach. We found this to no avail and as a last resort a third bombing run was made another 120 degrees from the previous two. Again, no luck.

Now it became obvious that we must consider making our attack on the secondary target, Nagasaki.

7. 8 SWEENEY 1997

What follows next are some quotes from WAR'S END: An Eyewitness Account of America's Last Atomic Mission, the nearly 300-page monograph by Charles W. Sweeney with James A. Antonucci and Marion K. Antonucci, who was also on board the plane carrying the atomic bomb. The following quotes have been taken from his account of the Nagasaki mission, from departure to attack. C. W. Sweeney was a Major in the Army at the time of the sortie, and he had accompanied Enola Gay on the sortie to Hiroshima three days earlier as captain of The Great Artiste.

At the start of the account, he describes the change of the plane carrying the atomic bomb to BOCK'S CAR after returning from the sortie to Hiroshima.

> *I had already decided that because all the delicate measuring instruments we had carried on the Hiroshima mission were still installed in my airplane, The Great Artiste, it made no sense to have the ground crews and technicians work through the day to remove the instruments, reinstall them in another B-29, and then recalibrate them. Instead, I would take Fat Man in Fred Bock's airplane, the Bock's Car, with my crew, and he would fly the Great Artiste, with his crew.*
>
> *However, on August 8, I would fly the Great Artiste one more time before the mission. The scientists were finally ready with a new improved fuse.*

> *At mid-morning I arrived at the initial point to commence the bomb run. Beahan activated the thirty-second tone signal. Just as we would do the next day when the tone stopped, Kermit yelled, "Bomb away," and I took the airplane into a sharp 155-degree turn. The bomb raced in its forward arc toward the designated altitude of 1,890 feet. A puff of smoke plumed into the sun-drenched tropical sky. The fuse had detonated. The inert pumpkin plopped harmlessly into the ocean.*

The test, we later learned from the scientists, had been successful. I guess that was good news, considering that in less than twenty-four hours we would be taking the actual bomb—fuses and all—on board with us to Japan.

Although I do not know the details of the B-29's serviceability and operational procedures, it seems like this string of missions using The Great Artiste was practically an abuse of the plane. The Great Artiste seems to have participated in the nuclear attack on Hiroshima, but is it true that it also flew to Nagasaki, whether in a leading or supporting role? From a layman perspective, one would think that the aircraft underwent significant strain during its first trip to Japan and back, and it must have needed time for maintenance before the next sortie.

Also, the fact that they had to test the fuses, a very important component, the day before the attack suggests an odd nonchalance for an operation involving a nuclear attack that would cost $2 billion to execute.

Sweeney refers to Pulitzer Prize Winner W. L. Laurence as "Bill Laurence", saying of him,

"He expressed disappointment at not being allowed to accompany Tibbets to Hiroshima, but was excited about being aboard for this mission. He would fly with Fred Bock. Not knowing that Fred and I had switched airplane, he thought I was my own, The Great Artiste, and so in his eyewitness account identified it as the strike aircraft, an error that would persist for many years after the war."

As I have said several times already, such a last-minute change of model seems odd for an operation that one would expect to be meticulously planned, given its $2 billion cost.

The drop method is discussed as follows:

> *As we had practiced, our approach to the target and release would be from 30,000 feet (9,000 meters). The bomb had to be dropped visually—no radar. The bombardier would have to see the target, even though a radar drop could be almost as accurate and effective.*

And on the briefing held before the mission, the following:

> *We were reminded in no uncertain terms to drop only visually, which was a natural introduction to the weather report.*

This seems somewhat at odds with what Commander Ashworth wrote about the authority given to the "Weaponer" to switch to radar targeting in the event that it proved necessary to complete the drop.

He wrote the following about the rendezvous scene over Yakushima Island:

> *At 30,000 feet, we arrived at the rendezvous at 7:45 A.M. on the button . Yakoshima was visible through breaks in the clouds. We had been flying for almost five hours through bad weather in complete radio silence. Within moments, Fred Bock appeared on my right wing. A few minutes passed, but there was no sign of Hopkins.*

In the end, two planes met at Yakushima and flew on to Kokura, but Navy Lt. Col. Ashworth, who was on board, wrote of the other plane that was able to join them, "*[we flew towards Kokura] with the hope that our companion B-29 was the one we wanted.*" In other words, he said he wasn't even sure if the other plane was Bock's plane or not. Examining the details, the descriptions of the two people who were supposed to be in the same plane together are slightly different.

Next is a quote from the scene describing Army Major Sweeney's approach to Kokura. It is a bit lengthy, but it offers a strong basis for the story that

Kokura was the primary target, so it is important to understand. Just a word of warning, this is *not* the script of the 1990 British movie "Memphis Belle."

> *Kokura lay ahead. Jim Van Pelt had picked it up on his radar screen a few minutes earlier. It was 9:45 A.M. The skies were still hazy, as reported earlier, but they were now mixed with broken clouds.*
>
> *As we arrived at the IP, some landmarks were reasonably visible—the river, buildings, even streets and parks—so we thought here was a good chance to sight the target, the Kokura arsenal.*
>
> *I started our bomb run when Beahan suddenly yelled, "I can't see it! I can't see it! There's smoke obscuring the target."*
>
> *The fires resulting from the bombing of Yahata the night before were still burning out of control, and heavy smoke was being drifted across Kokura by winds that had shifted direction since George Marquart had radioed his weather report.*
>
> *As we bore in on the aiming point, Beahan repeated, "I can't see it!" The great Kokura arsenal was safely hidden by the smoke and haze.*
>
> *I yelled into my intercom, "No drop. Repeat, no drop."*
>
> *I banked the airplane sharply to the left and swung around to the south to begin a return approach to the IP. Flak bursts started all around us—to the left, ahead, to the right, and behind us.*
>
> *A moment later tail gunner Pappy Dehart yelled, "Flak! Wide, but altitude is perfect." Everyone saw it.*
>
> *"Roger that, Pappy," I replied. There were crawling the flak up toward us as they tried to zero in on our airplane. I was now doing something a bomber pilot rarely, if ever, does—making a second run on a target. Second runs gave antiaircraft guns second chances.*
>
> *I changed my altitude to 31,000 feet to try to confuse the enemy flak fusing. As I proceeded toward the aiming point, Pappy broke in again. "This damn flak is right on our tail and getting closer." His voice now sounded a note of panic.*

"Forget it, Pappy. We're on a bomb run," I said evenly, trying to keep my attention on the approach to the aiming point.

I waited for Beahan's signal that he could see the target. I hoped he had picked it up through a break in the smoke and haze. I hoped we could catch a break on this mission.

"I can't see it!" he yelled again.

I wheeled into another steep turn as I barked, "No drop. Repeat, no drop."

Ed Buckly, our radar operator, reported, "Major, Jap Zeros coming up. Looks like about ten."

I decided to take us up another 1,000 feet to try to throw the anti-aircraft gunners off again, and then approach from a different angle. Maybe from a different angle we might have a chance of finding a hole in the cover.

Beahan and Van pelt were frantically calculating the run approach data.

The bursts of flak were breaking very close to the airplane, causing it to jump.

The third run was no more successful than the first two. The aiming point was still obscured. Kuharek reported that our fuel situation was very critical. We had enough to get to our secondary target, Nagasaki, and make one run. But we wouldn't make it back to Okinawa, the closest American base. We would fall short by about fifty miles.

Ed Buckley broke in over the intercom, "Fighters below and climbing to meet us."

Jake Beser, who was monitoring Japanese radio frequencies, confirmed increased activity on the Japanese fighter-director bands.

I wasn't as concerned about the Zeros as I was about the flack. Like horseshoes and grenades, close might be good enough if a burst caught us just right. If we hung around any longer it would only be a matter of time.

Our gunner, Ray Gallagher, muttered into his intercom, "Let's get the hell out of here." Abe Spitzer, our radio operator, kept saying, "What about Nagasaki? What about Nagasaki?"

"Cut the chatter," I ordered sharply.

I again banked sharply to set us on a southerly direction toward our secondary target.

This statement by Army Major Sweeney is probably a fiction. There were only a few anti-aircraft guns that could shoot as high as 30,000 feet (9,000 meters) deployed in the whole of Japan at that time. In addition, the city of Yahata, adjacent to Kokura, was heavily damaged by a firebombing on the morning of August 8. Consequently, many citizens still remember the following day—August 9—but as a result of my interviews with people who knew the area at that time and my examination of various records, no one heard the roar of anti-aircraft fire or fighter planes taking off. In Japan at that time, a few B-29s flying over a city would only result in sirens being sounded at most, as cities had already lost the ability to intercept them.

Therefore, if this statement is true, the Japanese attempted to intercept Sweeney's B-29s because they recognized something special about them, something different from a reconnaissance flight. But in such a case, even if the B-29s switched to Nagasaki, at least some Zero fighters would have followed them, resulting in some sort of engagement en-route to Nagasaki. However, from his description, no such thing occurred.

Another issue is that both Ashworth and Sweeney say that the Yahata raid occurred the night before they targeted Kokura, but this is not correct: it took place on the morning of the previous day. Since 'the night before' would have been about half a day after the Yahata raid, they may have wanted to give the impression that the fires from the bombardment were still raging.

I will leave my comments here for now, and move on to a quote from "The Second Atomic Bombing: Nagasaki" by Navy Lieutenant Colonel Ashworth describing the events as the B-29s finally approached Nagasaki.

7.9 ASHWORTH AGAIN

As we laid our course to Nagasaki we did so with some confidence that we would have better luck there than we had at Kokura. After all, the weather reconnaissance aircraft had reported the skies clear over Nagasaki several hours earlier. But weather is a fickle friend at times like these and as we neared the target area it appeared certain that the city of Nagasaki would be completely covered by clouds. Must an approach and bomb release be made by radar this time? If it were to be required the decision would be made somewhat easier since our instructions permitted us to attack on radar if it would be impossible to get the bomb back to a friendly base. In view of the fuel situation I believed that there was no choice, the approach must be made on radar and the bomb released on the solution generated by the electronic bomb director. The Navigator, Maj. Van Pelt, was trained for this and I had confidence in his ability to make a successful attack. I felt that it was my responsibility to satisfy myself that we were indeed heading for Nagasaki and a quick look into the navigator's radar scope assured me of this fact. The city and the long narrow bay extending to the mouth of the Urakami River were clearly visible and easily identified. While the approach continued Lt. Barnes again tested the integrity of the bomb electronic components and found everything normal and ready to go. Earlier during the war I was briefly under the command of Commo. Ben H. Wyatt, U.S. Navy '17 who told me that under conditions of stress he operated with a sense of the motto "Fortune aids the bold." We were now testing that motto.

The approach continued with the navigator calling out to the bombardier the dropping angles generated by the electronic bomb director thus permitting him to follow the bombing approach with his Norden bomb sight. As we approached the target area we noted that what had appeared from a distance to be a solid overcast over the target was actually more nearly 50 percent cloud cover and an area of the ground started to become visible.

Then Maj. Beahan called out over the internal communication circuit, "I have the target, taking control." In about 20 seconds he called out, "Bomb away" and we felt the jolt as the 10,000-pound bomb left the aircraft. With a violent turn to the left and a shallow dive the aircraft sped away from the target area in anticipation of the arrival of the shock wave. There was a brilliant flash of light visible even through the almost opaque goggles everyone on board was wearing, and I knew that the bomb had detonated as anticipated and probably at the desired height of burst. (Shipmate, page 20)

The above quote states that the target area in Nagasaki was initially approached by radar and that the bombing was supposed to be conducted by an electronic bomb director, but as visibility became clear just before the bombing, the targeting method could be switched to the Norden bomb sight. I believe that the Norden bomb sight system requires the target to be visible well in advance—after all, is this not why the target could not be confirmed at Kokura? With this in mind, please read the following quotation from Sweeney's book, which describes the same bombing sequence.

7. 10 SWEENEY AGAIN

I couldn't believe my eyes. Nagasaki was obscured by 80 to 90 percent cumulus at 6,000 to 8,000 feet. A visual drop was improbable. We were approaching from the northwest and would arrive at the initial point in a few minutes. Kuharek confirmed again—we had enough fuel for a single bomb run.

I called Commander Ashworth forward and laid out the situation. He was in charge of the bomb; I was in command of the aircraft. If we didn't drop, we were out of options. We had about 300 gallons of fuel. If we stayed too long at Nagasaki by making a second bomb run, we might be forced to crash-land on the ground in Japan or in the ocean. If we didn't get a visual on our first run and then depart, we'd have to dump the bomb into the ocean.

I summed up quickly, "We haven't got the time or the fuel for more than one run. Let's drop it by radar. I'll guarantee we come within five hundred feet of the target." This was a commitment whose execution would be up to Ed Buckley, Kermit Beahan, and Jim Van Pelt. I didn't have time to consult with them, but I had supreme confidence in my radar man, bombardier, and navigator.

"I don't know, Chuck," Ashworth said.

"It's better than dropping it into the ocean.," I answered.

"Are you sure of the accuracy?" Ashworth pressed.

"I'll take full responsibility for this," I assured him.

Ashworth could see that my only reason for any consultation was an interest in interservice harmony.

From the IP, Van Pelt and Buckley started to coordinate the approach to the aiming point. The outline of the city appeared on the scopes in front of Van Pelt and Buckley. Buckley called out headings and precise closure rates to Beahan, who fed the data into the bombsight, all the while hoping for a break in the clouds.

I reminded the crew to put on their goggles. I decided to leave mine off so I could see what was doing.

We were thirty seconds from the bomb's release. The tone signal was activated and the bomb bay doors snapped open. Twenty-five seconds. Then Beahan yelled, "I've got it!"

I answered, "You own it."

Beahan had spotted a hole midway between the two great Mitsubishi armaments plants in the industrial valley. It was two miles north of the assigned point and away from the residential area, now shielded by the low hills beyond the coastal plain. He locked onto a racetrack reference point and made his adjustments, which were fed into the course direction indi-

cator on my panel, from which I adjusted the flight path as required. I was still flying the airplane manually to the release point. Earlier in the run, Beahan had caught a momentary glimpse of the assigned aiming point, but it would have disrupted the radar run if he took over. He reconsidered, hoping for a better view, which proved to fortuitous for us and the city below.

"Bombs away," Beahan shouted, and then quickly corrected himself. "Bomb away."

At the moment of release the airplane lurched upward, suddenly ten thousand pounds lighter. It was 11:01 A.M. The bomb bay doors snapped shut. I took us into a steep, diving, 155-degree turn to the left, in a north-easterly direction, to get away from the blast.

Time seemed suspended. As the seconds ticked by, I began to wonder if we had dropped a dud.

Then suddenly the entire horizon burst into a super brilliant white with an intense flash—more intense than Hiroshima. The light was blinding. A moment later, the first wave of superheated air began hitting us with unexpected force. The shock wave were more severe than those at Hiroshima. But the airplane was still handling fine.

7. 11 SEARCHING FOR THE TRUTH ABOUT THE NAGASAKI BOMBING

The above is the most important literature I have been able to find on the Nagasaki atomic bombing, from the New York Times article written immediately after the bombing in 1945 to Sweeney's 1997 book.

Among these are the reports of Ashworth, a Weaponer and Lieutenant Commander in the Navy, and Sweeney, a Captain and Major in the Army, who were on board the plane, are now recognized as true worldwide, including Japan.

But here is one thing for you to consider.

Why were such reports only released more than 40 years after the bombing?

Both men are ex-military, and while there are differences between the Army and the Navy, their pride oozes out of their writing. Are the discrepancies between their accounts due to the vagueness of their memories? Both men say that they personally ordered the nuclear bombing to be conducted by radar sight. However, since one of them must have given that order, the other is clearly lying.

When the nuclear bomb was dropped on Hiroshima, the target was successfully obtained by visual sighting. The second bombing, then, was the world's first successful bomb drop by radar sight. Perhaps both men want to be able to take credit for this success.

Another reason for these men publishing these writings 40 years after the fact may be that the crews involved in the nuclear bombings of Hiroshima and Nagasaki had by then reached old age. The nuclear bombing that devastated the Catholic "holy city" of Nagasaki, in particular, may have been seen as a liability, and these commanders sought to firm up the military's narrative as a precaution against the possibility that crew members might reveal top-secret information in their senility.

Notably, between the different views provided, there are two claims that neatly coincide.

One is that the Yahata air raid took place "at night" the day before, and thus, the smoke from ongoing conflagration had covered Kokura.

However, the Yahata air raid had already taken place in the morning of the previous day, 24 hours before the bombing.

The other is the dramatic statement that just before the nuclear bombs were dropped, clouds suddenly opened up and visual sighting was made possible. This scene is very similar to one in the 1990 British film "The Memphis Belle," which makes one wonder if there is a connection.

Regardless, these stories both claim that were clouds in the sky at 10:00 a.m. on August 9, 1995. Walking along the Nagasaki Road in Kokura's Kinkeichō district, I looked up at that sky, pondering this.

What exactly were these clouds that covered the Kokura Arsenal?

Kinkeichō is a district that lies between Yahata and Kokura. If the smoke from the August 8 Yahata air raid fire covered Kokura, it would have covered this area as well. However, it seemed extremely doubtful to me that such a large volume of smoke could have drifted yet another 8 kilometers to cover the vast Kokura Arsenal, which covers an area of 176,000 tsubo (144 acres). I doubt that the scope of this scene could be easily depicted even by the use of cutting-edge computer graphics.

As a result, I became a believer in the theory that some of the conventional bombs that targeted Yahata on August 8 missed their targets and fell near the Kokura Arsenal, and it was the smoke from these bombs that covered it. According to Japanese records, incendiary bombs also fell near Kyushu Dental College, which is located near my clinic. This naturally led me to believe that some bombs also fell on the town of Kinkeichō, and as inappropriate as it was, I began to feel like a character in some drama, wondering if my own hometown was somehow involved in the Nagasaki bombing as well. For a while, I was caught up in this theory.

However, when I encountered a United States military report stating that only a small number of bombs missed their targets and fell on Kokura, such that they could not have produced nearly enough smoke to cover the arsenal in its vastness, I began to question the truth behind these clouds once more.

The B-29s that carried out the first strategic bombing on Yahata on June 15, 1944 took off from the Chengdu area of China. Their bombing accuracy was low, and they took massive damage due to enemy engagement. However, in the course of switching their attack base to the islands of Saipan, Tinian, and Guam in the Mariana Sea and embracing a strategy of using incendiary bombs to burn down the homes of huge numbers of civilians, the firebombers developed a perverse sense of pride in believing that they were the main players in bringing an end to the war: they would be the ones who would finish off the Japanese. However, their pride was shattered on August 6. Stories of the B-29 Special Strike Group, returning to base after a successful nuclear attack on Hiroshima, would have spread throughout Tinian overnight. The star role had shifted to the nuclear bombing squadrons, and those who merely scattered conventional incendiary bombs had been reduced to minor players.

The small number of bombs that missed their targets and fell on Kokura during the Yahata air raid on August 8 may not have "missed" at all, but were rather due to conventional bombers violating orders out of a sense of wounded pride. They may have been trying to restore their wounded pride by destroying munitions facilities, which should have been the original purpose of the bombing, rather than killing civilians.

I was told by a senior member of a medical association who actually experienced the air raid that on August 8 that there were some projectiles that were clearly aimed specifically at housing complexes scattered across the region from Takami to Saigatani, a few kilometers away from the target area of the Yahata air raid. Apparently, the accuracy of their strikes was astonishing. Perhaps the bombers thought that they could demonstrate their skills better than in areas where the bombs were being dropped more densely.

On the eve of the Yahata air raid, a warning leaflet was distributed by air from a U.S. military plane, claiming that the same powerful bomb that was dropped on Hiroshima would be dropped again on August 8, warning civilians to evacuate the area. The content of such leaflets may have been deliberately misleading to conceal the true target of the nuclear attack.

8. CLOUDS

Let's backtrack a moment.

Again: what in the world were these supposed clouds that covered Kokura Arsenal?

My father volunteered to become a naval pre-commissioned officer at the end of the war. He wanted to be a fighter pilot, like Peter Townsend, but no fighter planes were available at the time. I believe he later volunteered to be a member of the Shin-yō motorboat suicide attack team, but the war ended with his assignment to a suicide attack base in Uwajima. Although he won't confirm it, according to what I have heard, he and his comrades made a blood pact on the eve of the war's end, saying, "If the Americans come ashore, we'll take them out!" In fact, there was one incident in Kochi Prefecture suicide base , located in the immediate vicinity of Uwajima on August 16 where the Shin-yō Corps attempted to launch a sortie. This is the site at which the "Memorial Tower for the Martyrs of the Shin-yō Corps" was built (from the Wikipedia article on Shin-yō [Suicide Boats]).

Fortunately, my father was blessed with a kind-hearted superior officer and was able to survive.

Perhaps because I was born to such a father, my interest in the war was strong from an early age, and I read through my father's vast collection of war-related books. My interest and knowledge earned me the title of "Junior Chief of Staff" from an officer of the Japan Maritime Self-Defense Force while I was in elementary school.

At one point, I had a bit of a realization.

It had to do with the great naval battle centering on Leyte Island in the Philippines in October 1944. The Battleship Musashi had already been sunk, and the last of the Imperial Japanese Navy's giant battleships, led by the Battleship Yamato, were about to enter the Leyte Gulf, the target of their attack. They happened to encounter a carrier fleet escorting an American landing force, which they tried to destroy by concentrating fire on it. The U.S. escort carrier force, fleeing from the overwhelming difference in firepower (compared to the power of the main U.S. carrier fleet), was fortunate enough to be hidden by clouds in a nearby squall, giving them a smokescreen that obstructed the visual fire of the Japanese. Smokescreens and clouds are ineffective against radar sighting, but the accuracy of Japanese radar fire at that time was very poor, and the American forces escaped with little damage. The Japanese mistakenly believed that they had destroyed the "main carrier fleet" at that time, which proved to be an error of dark foreshadowing.

Even at sea, ships can interfere with visual sighting with smokescreens. I thought that there was no way that one of Japan's leading military industrial bases could have failed to make such preparations in case of an enemy air raid.

So, I entered the three keywords "Kokura," "atomic bomb," and "smoke screen" into an Internet search. Then I found a publication under the top hits. The title of the book was "The Atomic Bombing Operation, Seen from the Side." The author was Miyako Akiyoshi, who was an elementary school student in the Chikuhō region near Yahata at the end of the war, and her description was well-written. Reading this book, I felt as if I had finally grasped the true nature of the clouds. The Kokura Arsenal had put up a smokescreen before the B-29s carrying atomic bombs approached!

I came to believe that the Kokura Arsenal, upon receiving reports that B-29s were approaching Kyushu on August 9, recognized that an attack like the one on Hiroshima was imminent, and had the Japanese Army and Navy ready to intercept the B-29s, while they themselves put up a smokescreen. Because of this defensive posture, a nuclear attack on Kokura was averted, but Nagasaki was sacrificed instead. Therefore, the officers who ordered this smokescreen operation may have remained silent after the war in lamentation and concealed the fact that they had successfully defended themselves.

However, if it is true that they avoided the atomic bombing by putting up a smokescreen, one would expect some kind of folklore around this incident to remain. Since the smokescreen supposedly covered the entire arsenal grounds, about 57,000m²(144acres), many people must have been involved, and smoke must have been billowing out of dozens of chimneys. No matter how much the authorities tried to cover up the fact, there should be at least one legend about that day among the people of Kokura.

In reality, there are no such legends. On sober analysis, the probability of the smokescreen theory being true is quite low.

I conducted this internet search in 2009.

In order to write "Revive The Bells of Nagasaki!," I conducted another internet search in 2019, entering the three keywords "Kokura," "atomic bomb," and "smokescreen." This time, Akiyoshi's publication was much further down in the hits, while an article from the front page of the July 26, 2014 Mainichi News Paper came to the forefront. It described an incident on August 9, 1945, in which an employee of the former Yahata Steel Works burned coal tar to put up a smokescreen in preparation for the coming of the B-29s. The person said that after the war, he had always been tormented by a sense of guilt that his actions may have contributed to the planes switching their target from Kokura to Nagasaki. The article included a claim from an "expert" that the Yahata Steel Works smokescreen theory cannot be overlooked as a way to explain the poor visibility over Kokura; this claim attracted attention overseas.

If I could meet the "expert" who commented for this Mainichi News Paper article, I'd like to say to him or her the following:

"For years since the war ended, ordinary people have struggled with their thoughts and feelings about what they experienced, and now they are revealing those long-hidden memories. However, it is the role of "experts" such as yourself to carefully examine the truthfulness of what they say and what they mean. As a resident of Kokura, I can tell you that it would have been very difficult, even for someone in the town, to cover the entirety of Kokura Arsenal with a smokescreen. There is no way anyone could have done it from Yahata, which is quite some distance from Kokura. Is not the common-sense conclusion that, because some B-29s flew over Yahata the day after the air raid, someone rushed to pump out smoke from the chimneys in an effort to protect the steelworks? Isn't it more likely that this person heard about the bombing in Nagasaki after the war and assumed that their own actions had something to do with it, causing them to feel guilty ever since?"

This former Yahata Steel Works employee received so much attention that he was featured in a TV program in 2015, but in the last five years, he has not been mentioned. The mainstream story has shifted to saying that what covered the skies of Kokura on August 9 was combustion smoke from the Yahata air raid. Ironically, however, creating enough smoke from an explosion to also cover Kokura, 10 kilometers away, *itself* would have required the dropping of a nuclear bomb.

9. THE SILENT DAY

So, I ask again: those clouds that supposedly covered the arsenal - what were they?

Was it really combustion smoke from the Yahata air raid?

I published this very "head in the clouds" story in the "Kitakyushu Medical Association Bulletin" that I make available in the waiting room of my clinic. A patient who read it asked me to make some time for him because he really needed to talk to me about something.

The patient's name was Yukio Komatsu.

He was a former employee of Kitakyushu City and was in the fifth grade of junior school at the end of WWII.

He told me that he clearly remembered the events of August 9, 1945, because in the evening of that day, one of his classmates was severely beaten by a teacher and died the next day, searing the date into his memory. Nowadays, such an incident would make national news, but back then, such things may have been rather commonplace.

What follows is his account.

Shortly after 8:00 a.m. on the morning of August 9, the first siren sounded, and I slowly headed toward the recessed evacuation shelter dug into the cliffs along the Itabitsu River in Shimoitouzu. Even though it was summer, the shelter was too cold for me due to water leakage, so I went outside. When I did so, I saw a B-29 flying overhead; it looked to be about the size of a hawk. I figured that it was a reconnaissance flight, and since the alarm was lifted at around 8:15, I prepared to go help dig trenches at Sarayama.

A second siren sounded, which was soon replaced by an air raid alarm. Not wanting to go into that cold shelter again, I stood on the river bank and looked toward the city. Two B-29s were flying above clouds that looked like spread-out cotton. They were not dropping bombs or incendiary bombs, just circling over and over again. All the while, I didn't hear a single shot from an anti-aircraft gun, not a puff of smoke from a shell bursting in the air. There was no sign of the fighter planes that, at the height of the war, had slammed into the B-29s in furious, doomed resistance, sending everyone on the ground into a frenzy.

Frankly, I was more concerned about when the sale of meal tickets for substitute meals would start at the Okisada Cafeteria facing the train station in Itouzu. Once the air raid alarm alerted us that the B-29s were gone, I hurried to the cafeteria, but I didn't make it in time and had to go without lunch. If the alarm had lasted until noon, we would have gotten the day off from school, but since it lifted by 11:00, I had no choice but to follow the school's instructions and help out with the trenches. A teacher made a number of students stand in a line because they were "far too tardy" and, to make an example of them, punched one of them in the face. The student fell backward and remained motionless for some time. In the evening, he managed to return home, but died the next morning.

Mr. Komatsu remembered the events of August 9 long after the war. As it became clearer and clearer what had happened in Nagasaki that day, and after he heard the story about Kokura being the first target of the atomic bombing, he wrote a detailed account of the events of that day. He has been pursuing the meaning of his memories for 60 years. That is why, after he came across my writings in the waiting room of my clinic, he was so insistent on sharing his thoughts with me.

Mr. Komatsu describes a quiet sky at around 10:00 a.m. on August 9, when two B-29s came to Kokura and circled "above clouds that looked like spread-out cotton," without any anti-aircraft gunfire or fighter interception. The clouds were likely cumulus, a type of cloud that appears at altitudes of up to 2,000 meters; the B-29s would have been flying at an altitude of around 3,000 meters (10,000 feet). Incidentally, when the atomic bomb was dropped on Nagasaki, the altitude of the B-29 was 9,000 meters. At that height, its shadow would likely have looked no larger than a mosquito.

I would like to introduce another important testimony.

The following is a quote from "A Medical Student's War Diary" by Dr. Eiki Kagawa, who was a student at the Kokura Prefectural Medical and Dental School at the time.

At about 10:00 a.m. on August 9, 1945, Shinkawa [the protagonist] was evacuated into a tunnel for two hours, but no bombing took place, there was no anti-aircraft fire, and no friendly aircraft interception appeared. Dr. Toshio Nagata, his classmate, also testified that "there was no anti-aircraft fire or interception from our own planes. It was quiet."

Whether they were optimists or fools, Shinkawa and the others kept moving in and out of the narrow tunnel dugout, then looked up at the sky.

"I heard that a large bomb was dropped on Hiroshima. I heard it did a lot of damage. I heard that a rescue team was organized from the affiliated hospital and dispatched to the city. Is this the end of Japan?"

"What's going to happen to us?" Clearly, we were all a bit at wit's end.

But there is something else that must be mentioned.

Back then, I had only looked up at the sky for what must have been around 20 seconds. For many years, I could not determine if this was fact or my own fantasy, but I remember seeing two silver B-29s flying over the gap between the clouds.

It was the third time they had invaded the skies.

Dr. Nagata testified, "I saw two B-29s in the gap in the clouds, seemingly about 60 centimeters in size. They were flying in the direction of Yahata City (towards Nagasaki City)."

The cloud layer at that time was between 1,800 and 2,400 meters high. The planes must have appeared that size because they were flying another 3,000 meters or more above the cloud level.

This account, consisting of Dr. Kagawa's recollections and the testimony of his friend, Dr. Nagata, roughly agrees with Mr. Komatsu's earlier description of two B-29s circling at an altitude of about 3,000 meters. In fact, both of these people believe that these B-29s were carrying atomic bombs. Both of them are intellectually gifted people, and I think that their assessment of the altitude is likely correct. However, if an atomic bomb were dropped at that altitude, the bomber would be blown to pieces by the blast from the ground. I doubt that a nuclear bomb would ever have been dropped from this altitude, because the U.S. military never orders its soldiers to carry out suicide attacks.

So, did B-29s carrying atomic bombs really fly over Kokura?

To recap the story given by the U.S. military, B-29s carrying the atomic bombs took off from Tinian in a formation of three planes, but one of the planes made a careless mistake by getting separated at Yakushima Island. By the time it had arrived at Kokura, the clouds over the army arsenal had become thick. This delayed the bombing mission, and during their three attempts to drop the bomb, the plane was exposed to Japanese anti-aircraft guns and interceptors. Out of a concern that the plane carrying the bomb might be shot down, the target was finally changed to Nagasaki.

I met with and interviewed a representative of the Kitakyushu Association for Documenting the War in Kitakyushu, who had conducted a detailed interview-based investigation about the Yahata air raid of August 8, 1945. I asked him if smoke really flowed from Yahata to cover the Kokura Arsenal on August 9. He replied as follows:

"Yes, smoke from the Yahata air raid did cover Kokura. We know this based on statements made by the U.S. military in its postwar investigative records."

Even though the group to which this person belongs is presumably ideologically critical of the United States, there was still a willingness on his part to believe what the US said.

I pushed him further..

"Then, did anyone actually witness that smoke stream? Did you encounter even one person who made such testimony?"

He replied, "Well, I have heard many people talk about it, but I have never been able to find any direct testimony to that effect, no."

Mr. Shigeto Yanagihara, who was a 13-year-old student at a technical high school student at the time of the Yahata air raid, testified as follows:

> *"So, the idea is that Kokura was spared from the atomic bombing because of the smoke in Yahata from the previous day.*
>
> *The town of Yahata had been destroyed so completely in the air raid that there wasn't even anything left to burn by the next day. Things were still smoking, yes, but it wasn't filling up the sky. On the way back home, I saw how the wood was burnt and black and charcoal-like, and the coke that was left all over the place was still burning with enough intensity to power a blast furnace. Once coke is lit, it keeps burning until there's nothing left. But there wasn't enough smoke to cover the sky the next day."*

This testimony is included in the book "What Happened in Yahata That Day: 70 Years after the Yahata Air Raid," which was carefully compiled by Kitakyushu City. His description of the incident is credible, given that he was 13 years old at the time and was engaged in industrial work in the following years.

Considering such testimony, does it not seem as though the story of the smoke that covered the Kokura Arsenal may, in fact, have been a fabrication of the U.S. military?

My father used to reminisce about his days as a pre-commissioned officer when he drank and would often say, "I'd still be willing to attack America with a bomb in my hand. That's how I was raised, I can't help it."

But once, when he was sober, he said the following:

"The Americans conquered the Native Americans, taking over the vast North American continent. They're not just talented strategists, they're strong, too. What were we thinking, attacking a nation like that? No wonder we lost so badly."

The atomic bombing was a massive undertaking and apparently cost one-third of the U.S. national budget. It is hard to believe that the United States, a scientific society that is both ferocious and meticulous when it comes to "warfare," would have made such a careless mistake as to let the smoke from their own bombs interfere with their nuclear attack the next day, or letting one of their planes get separated during rendezvous.

There's an even simpler issue here.

If the bombers were preparing to drop a nuclear bomb on Kokura, they would have needed to open the jacket of the plutonium bomb itself. However, the difference in complexity between the uranium bomb that was dropped on Hiroshima and the plutonium bomb is like the difference in complexity between a bicycle and an automobile. That's how much simpler the structure of the uranium bomb was, but even that bomb required a very complicated procedure to prepare for the drop. Once the bomb jacket was opened, it would not have been easy to close again. It would have been impossible to close the jacket again for the plutonium bomb, which required an even more complicated procedure, and then head for Nagasaki.

In fact, Major Sweeney's book at one point mentions that the bomb bay doors were snapped open, but this only occurred just before the Nagasaki bombing, not while the planes were flying over Kokura (quoted in 62 page of this book).

There is also uncertainty regarding the target sighting. It is not clear what the precise target in Kokura was supposed to be.

According to Yozo Kudo and others who have studied the atomic bombings in detail, in the U.S. military's field orders for the atomic bombings published after the war, the sighting target for the Hiroshima attack was "Aioi Bridge (river width 120 meters)," and for Nagasaki, "Megane Bridge (river width 20 meters)". It seems that large bridges such as the Aioi Bridge were often chosen as sighting points for bombing cities because they were easy to see when using visual sights along a straight, horizontal bombing line tens of kilometers away, as they could be identified as straight lines crossing rivers. In the case of Nagasaki, the Nakajima River, which is about 20 meters wide, curves inland from its outlet into Nagasaki Bay and then straightens out. Megane Bridge crosses right about at the point where the river straightens. While the bridge itself is small and difficult to see, if one follows the course of the river, visual sighting should be possible. Kokura, however, has an enormous number of bridges; a certain former mayor "Mr. Bridge" built so many bridges that he attracted criticism for the practice. The sighting point couldn't have been much more specific than "one of the bridges or close to it." Kudo's research also does not offer clarification on this.

Together, these factors suggest that the U.S. forces never had any plan to bomb Kokura.

The three-plane atomic bombing squadron that departed from Tinian probably did not go to Kokura at all.

The B-29s flying over Kokura may well have been two completely separate units. If not, why would such a complex plan be necessary?

It must have taken a considerable amount of time with the technology back then to ensure that the implosion-type nuclear bombs, with all their complex mechanisms, would explode at the designated altitude after being dropped by the planes that took off from Tinian. Therefore, the dropping team may have simply continued circling over Yakushima Island, only heading for Nagasaki once the preparations were complete.

10. THE TRUTH ABOUT AMERICA —THE SOVIET THREAT

Everyone knows that the war ended on August 15, 1945, when Japan, the last holdout of the Tripartite Pact, surrendered. Will future generations of historians be able to explain why it took until August 15? Why did it not end on April 7, 1945, when the sinking of the Battleship Yamato marked the end of the Japanese Navy? Why did it not end on June 23, 1945, when the Japanese Army collapsed after their defeat in the Battle of Okinawa, when Japan should have immediately surrendered?

I consider the atomic bombing of Nagasaki and the entry of the Soviet Union into the war against Japan on August 9 to be the first day of the Cold War. From that day forward, an unprecedented insanity began to spread across the globe: the theory of nuclear deterrence. Russia's recent invasion of Ukraine, which began on February 24, 2022, has reminded us all that it is still not yet behind us.

After World War I, countries frantically began expanding their conventional arsenals, until finally, restrictions on the production of battleships and other warships were established by the so-called "disarmament" pact of the Washington Naval Treaty (1922). The treaty established a ratio cap for battleships between the signatories, at 5:5:3 for Britain, the United States, and Japan. Japan responded by increasing its number of aircraft carriers and submarines to compensate for the discrepancy, eventually withdrawing from the League of Nations. On the eve of the Pacific War against US, Japan was said to boast the world's strongest navy. In contrast, the U.S. Navy seemed to lack such naval power at the opening of the Pacific Theater.

I get the sense that the United State may have already begun working towards a shift to nuclear hegemony by this stage. Presumably, in preparation for possible conflict, there would have been rampant spy activity, with a great deal of information on naval capabilities passing back and forth across the Pacific. One would expect the U.S., having an accurate grasp of Japanese naval power, to augment its own naval power in response. In reality, however, the war began in Japan's favor, with its surprise attack on Pearl Harbor (1941). But perhaps the attack was within U.S. intelligence expectations. While the Japanese had been fighting with conventional weapons throughout the war, the development of nuclear weapons was already underway. Once nuclear arms were successfully developed, the war changed dramatically. A single bomb could obliterate a fleet or destroy an entire division, making it a tactical weapon of unimaginable power.

After the end of World War I in 1918, the highest echelons of the U.S. military anticipated the scientific and technological advances yet to come in aircraft, ships, and weapons, while simultaneously looking ahead to the changing world framework and the persistent belligerence of the times. It is believed that the U.S. military was among the first to recognize the potential for nuclear-science-based tactical weapons in the large-scale conflicts of a second world war, and probably began researching their development in secret as early as the 1920s. This analysis is based on the timeline of development of the Norden visual sight system, which is capable of tracking strategic targets from an altitude of 9,000 meters (30,000 feet) and which was already being researched by this time at enormous cost.

In 1934, the U.S. also began development of a bomber capable of carrying a large number of bombs while flying at high altitude, at similarly great expense. This culminated in the B-29, completed in June 1943.

Of course, other countries, including Japan, were aware that it was theoretically possible to produce a weapon of destruction using nuclear energy that would possess such power as to dwarf gunpowder, and it seems that a number of countries were engaged in their fair share of research and investigation.

Nonetheless, among them, only the United States succeeded in overcoming the many challenges involved in the development of nuclear weaponry. Certainly, the American super rich, who owned industrial conglomerates were astonishingly tenacious in their attempts to make the US the premiere national power, as well as holding the world's greatest economy, education, and intellectual level, by any means necessary. Certainly, they showed no hesitation in starting wars in pursuit of personal profit. However, I believe that a certain religious passion for "world domination" was at the root of the U.S. success in developing nuclear weapons, and zealots of this demonic religion were indispensable to it. I believe that it was the black passion of these hidden, powerful leaders that led to the atomic bombing of Japan, which was carried out as an elaborate and daring secret program under the direct control of the U.S. president, at a cost of $3 billion and with the efforts of 130,000 people.

It is often said that world-class scientists such as Einstein lobbied the leaders of the United States to develop nuclear weapons in order to counter Nazi Germany's development of nuclear weapons and protect the world from fascism, based on information that Nazi Germany was developing such weapons themselves. The story goes that, while the development of nuclear weapons in Nazi Germany ended up falling behind, the use of nuclear weapons on Japan hastened the end of the war and prevented many human losses. I find these stories very difficult to believe.

As outlined by world-renowned physicist Dr. Joseph Rotblat, the discovery and successful experimentation of nuclear fission was announced in January 1938. Nuclear fission is when a neutron strikes a nucleus, the nucleus splits, simultaneously releasing a number of neutrons. When the released neutrons further strike the surrounding nucleus, the nucleus splits again, releasing multiple neutrons. If this chain reaction of fission were to occur in a very short period of time, the most advanced scientists of the time predicted that it would produce an explosion of unprecedented power, generating an enormous amount of energy.

What would happen if Nazi Germany succeeded in developing an atomic bomb that utilized that fission? Anxiety spread among the world's leading scientists, including Einstein, that Hitler must surely use the atomic bomb, based on the theory of world domination that he had openly advocated. They then wrote to the leaders of the United States to urge them to develop nuclear weapons in order to counter the Nazis. In response, the U.S. leaders proceeded with their study, and in October 1942, they launched the Project for the Development of Nuclear Weapons, the so-called "Manhattan Project," and succeeded in developing a nuclear bomb in less than three years.

Although Einstein's letter seems to have been the major impetus for the start of the U.S. nuclear development, the Manhattan Project was actually launched three years after Einstein's letter. In fact, during that time, basic research for the development of nuclear weapons was vigorously conducted in the United Kingdom, and it was only when the scientific prospects for the realization of an atomic bomb had been established that the United States made its move.

The U.S. military must have already had information that nuclear development in Germany was impossible at the time the Manhattan Project was launched. However, they must have kept it a secret to keep many of their scientists and engineers motivated to develop nuclear weapons. In order to dominate the Soviet Union and achieve world domination in secret, the U.S. leaders proceeded with the development of nuclear weapons on the assumption that they would actually be used against Japan.

Besides, it is hard to imagine that the development of nuclear weapons, a process that requires unimaginably high levels of intelligence and technology, could be completed in a period of time as short as five to six years. I believe that there are many hidden truths about the development and use of nuclear weapons that differ wildly from the information that is publicly available. Officially, it is said that fission, the mechanism behind nuclear explosions, was discovered in late 1938 and published in January of the following year, but I suspect that a secret U.S. military laboratory must have discovered the tremendous destructive potential of nuclear fission long before that.

In the last years of his life, Einstein said that if he had to do it over again, he would have chosen a different profession such as tinsmith, peddler, or lighthouse keeper. One anecdote claims that, after hearing that the atomic bomb was dropped on the citizens of Hiroshima, Einstein cried out that if he had known that they were going to do that, he would not have become a scientist.

At any rate, it was not Japan, but the Soviet Union, that posed the greatest threat to the United States aims at "world domination." The perceived threat was ostensibly due to the need to suppress the false ideology of "communism" by "democratizing" the Soviet Union, which would lead to greater world happiness.

For the U.S., Japan's geographical location must have seemed a tantalizing outpost for attacking or checking the Soviet Union. I find it likely that they drew up a pincer scenario for the Soviet Union by putting Germany, which is located to the west of the Soviet Union, under their control as well.

In fact, as early as March 1944, Dr. Joseph Rotblat, a physicist involved in the development of U.S. nuclear weapons, was quoted by General Leslie Groves, who was in charge of the Manhattan Project, as saying, "The real objective of building the nuclear bomb is, of course, to subdue the Soviet Union!" At this time, thousands of Soviet soldiers were dying every day on the Eastern Front in order to defeat the German army and to buy time for the

Allied Powers to prepare for a landing on the European continent. When Dr. Rotblat heard General Groves' true intentions, his disgust at the treachery of the U.S. military establishment toward its ally motivated his decision to withdraw from the Manhattan Project, at great personal risk.

The very notion of a "nuclear weapon," a weapon of unspeakable cruelty and misery, is itself testament to how its development was a product of the most perverse corners of the human psyche. It is notable that, even in the midst of this madness, there were still people like Dr. Rotblat who came to their senses and walked away.

The fact that the U.S. pursued the development of two different types of nuclear bombs demonstrates a tremendous persistence, far beyond mere madness, to bring such weapons into being.

One of the bomb types was the "uranium bomb" or the gun-barrel-type. Not only is it extremely difficult to refine and enrich the uranium that it demands, but it requires tremendous effort even just to secure the nuclear material needed for a single bomb. However, the design of the bomb itself is straightforward, and will result in nuclear explosion as long as there is a sufficient amount of nuclear material. This is the type of bomb that was dropped on Hiroshima.

The other type was the "plutonium bomb" or the implosion-type for which it is relatively easy to secure nuclear raw materials, but the mechanism to cause a nuclear explosion is complex and requires an incredibly high degree of precision, making technological development extremely difficult. This is the type of bomb that was dropped on Nagasaki.

The uranium bomb, with its simple structure, could have been developed long before the end of the Pacific War, if only the technology for refining the raw material had been successfully developed - which is also quite difficult - after which, the only remaining obstacle would have been the substantial costs of procuring the raw material. Since the material could easily cause a nuclear explosion, but only one could be made, the timing and location of its use would have been planned in great detail to ensure maximum effectiveness.

In contrast, the plutonium bomb would have been extremely difficult to develop, but once successful, it would be possible to produce many more bombs, making it a powerful weapon in the war against the Soviet Union. Furthermore, its development was conducive to the further development of a hydrogen bomb, which, having thousands of times more destructive power, was expected to be a reliable a trump card against the Soviet Union, no matter how powerful a country it may be.

The United States likely thought that simply demonstrating the threat that nuclear weapons pose by dropping a uranium bomb–where only one bomb was needed–would be a major step toward United States world domination. If the U.S. military then succeeded in developing a plutonium bomb, they could spread a vision of nuclear weapons being used for widespread military force annihilation operations: a strategic coup for any military.

Unfortunate though it was, these efforts succeeded, and the world's first plutonium bomb test took place in the U.S. state of New Mexico on July 16, 1945: the Trinity Test.

11. THE STRATEGIC BOMBINGS

As I said previously, when I was in elementary school, I was so familiar with the Pacific War (The battle between Japan and the U.S. in World War II), that an active officer of the Japan Maritime Self-Defense Force dubbed me the "Junior Chief of Staff." There were probably not many elementary school students in Japan at the time who had such extensive knowledge of the war. Given my long-standing interest on the topic, I'd like to give an overview of my speculation over the last 50 years.

The reasons for Japan's defeat in the war are said to be various, such as the difference in air power, oil, and strategic materials, the neglect of logistics and search and rescue, the emphasis on attack, the outdated 'big ships and big guns' doctrine, the arrogance of the Japanese military, sloppy information management, the discord between the Army and Navy, underhanded tactics, etc. How true is any of this, really?

What if, after the end of World War I, in the 1920s, Japanese leaders had calmly assessed the mood in America and recognized its ambition for world domination? In order to check the Soviet Union and to mount a full defense against the U.S. attacking from the east, Japan would have needed to establish friendly relations with Korea and China. Mobile naval forces would have needed to be deployed primarily to secure southern routes for oil. In addition, to strengthen maritime defense, it would have been necessary to enhance its huge battleship force and air force escort. The United States is a country that is extremely sensitive to the sacrifice of its own citizens. If Japan had stuck to a defensive posture, the country would have been a nearly impenetrable fortress. In fact, on the eve of the outbreak of the Pacific War, the Japanese Navy was in just such a position.

I believe that what actually led to defeat in the Pacific War was Japan's own aggression, by initiating war with the U.S. with its attack on Pearl Harbor.

It is often said that the Japanese Navy, which was considered the strongest in the world at the beginning of the war in 1941, was more than capable of containing the U.S. and British navies, but that the defeat at the Battle of Midway had a major impact on the subsequent outcome of the war.

I think the movie "Midway", produced in America in 2019, is a good film about this battle. It offers a very balanced portrayal with different perspectives, unlike older films. This naval battle was the first and last time the Japanese and American forces fought to the death on equal terms using conventional weapons. It left the impression that, if possible, further advances in weaponry should be halted. While war is always cruel and tragic, this especially intense battle demonstrated the absolute limit of violent conflict that can still maintain some lingering sense of humanity. In that sense, the film offers a hard line by which we can deny the legitimacy of nuclear weapons as human tools–even for war.

What would have happened if Japan had won the Battle of Midway, giving them the advantage?

Japan likely still would not have been able to defeat the U.S. forces. It would have been absolutely impossible for Japan to conquer or hold the massive landmass of North America. Moreover, the entire country of the United States was nearing completion of nuclear weapons and their delivery technology. The longer the Pacific War dragged on, the more advanced that the nuclear weapons and their delivery systems would have become, with a single nuclear bomb being enough to destroy a major Japanese military base.

At some point, however, the "tactical use" of nuclear bombs apparently changed direction from strategic bombing to destroying large cities, from killing soldiers on battlefields to massacring civilians.

One of the factors that prompted this change in direction was the Japanese bombing of Chongqing, China, over a three-year period beginning in May 1939. Indiscriminate bombing from the air was pioneered by the Luftwaffe's bombing of Guernica in 1937, though it lasted only one day. The Italian Air Force also conducted tactical bombing of Ethiopian forces, albeit on a small scale.

On a scale unparalleled by these maneuvers, the Japanese forces launched a total of 218 sorties, killing a total of 11,885 Chinese civilians through bombings. The Japanese army's intention behind destroying a densely populated city that had nothing to do with the military advance was to increase the fear of the Chinese people as a whole, to incite war-weariness, and eventually to bring the Chinese to their knees. However, the bombings only served to inflame anti-Japanese sentiment among the Chinese people. Consequently, China began assisting the U.S. in staging bombings from the Chengdu area on Japan: against the nation that had perfected indiscriminate killing from the air. The U.S. military later moved its base to the Mariana Islands, where it carried out the widescale firebombing that culminated in the bombing of Hiroshima and Nagasaki.

The US interpreted Japan's National Mobilization Law of 1938 as providing the legal basis for the strategic bombings. This law stipulated that the government could mobilize all of the nation's human and material resources under its control for the conduct of total national warfare. Under this interpretation, the U.S. military recognized all citizens of Japan as "soldiers" involved in military operations. Hence, city dwellers, rural people, the young, the old, male or female, were all soldiers that could be legally killed. And killed they were, in endless fire bombings, by endless sorties of B-29s.

In the beginning of the Pacific War, U.S. forces were at a disadvantage after the surprise attack on Pearl Harbor, but overcame frictions between the Army and Navy early on to engage the formidable Japanese forces, gradually gaining the upper hand. Although it is often said that the U.S. forces overwhelmed the Japanese forces by sheer numbers, in reality, the difference in numbers was not initially all that great. Rather, the Army and Navy worked together, if sometimes at odds with each other, to confront Japan's powerful military. In contrast, the Japanese Army and Navy did not get along very well, and they were gradually driven into a corner by repeated failures caused by poor coordination. In the latter stages of the Pacific War, the U.S. forces were able to overpower the Japanese forces with conventional weapons alone, and as a result, targeting Japanese military facilities with nuclear bombs was no longer necessary to secure victory. In other words, in the end, there was no need to use such weapons at all.

Japan's strategic bombing of Chongqing and atrocities in East Asia became the target of world condemnation, which contributed to the U.S. military's assessment that the world would tolerate a nuclear attack on Japan. Under the slogan "Remember Pearl Harbor," the United States sought to gain the support of its populace by presenting its nuclear bombing campaign as an effort to exact revenge on "despicable Japan" for its surprise attack. Certainly, the Japanese military had given an aggressive United States an excellent pretext and opportunity. Moreover, the real purpose, as mentioned above, was to eventually bring the Soviet Union under its control. Unlike Japan, a large power like the Soviet Union could not have been directly subdued, no matter how many conventional weapons were deployed. Therefore, it could only be possible to suppress the Soviet Union by force if nuclear weapons could be used for intimidation or actual destruction. As a first step towards this goal, the U.S. president and the top echelons of the U.S. military must have decided that the use of nuclear bombs against Japan was geopolitically essential, while offering the public justification that the bombings would bring the Pacific War to a swift end.

In other words, the nuclear bombings were not the attacks. They were the test and the demonstrations.

12. THE INTERNAL COMBUSTION ENGINE

I have been involved in motorsports for 20 years.

Although I am not a good racer, I have been on the podium several times.

In September 2005, I participated in the Volkswagen GOLF GTI (VW) 100 km endurance race, a support race for the official International Formula 3 series race. There were three classes, the fastest being the latest Golf GTI-V with a 2,000cc 4-cylinder engine with an exhaust turbine supercharger and 200 horsepower output. Next was the Golf GTI3, a 2,000 cc naturally aspirated engine with 150 hp output, and third was the LUPO GTI, a 1,800 cc engine with 135 hp. I competed in the GTI-III class as a privateer.

Volkswagen's origins lie in a high-performance compact mass-market car designed by Dr. Ferdinand Porsche in the 1930s; commonly known as the Beetle. The development of the Beetle was realized in conjunction with Adolf Hitler's prewar populist policies, but with the outbreak of World War II, it was diverted to military use instead of being mass-produced for civilian use. It is likely that the rear air-cooled engine and rear-wheel-drive structure of the Beetle made it advantageous for escape when stuck in swampy areas during the invasion of the Soviet Union, and its excellent rough road drivability and serviceability attracted the attention of the German Army.

After the war, the Beetle became a huge hit, boasting a cumulative production record of more than 20 million units.

In 1974, the modern layout of the front water-cooled engine and front-wheel drive "Golf" was launched to replace the Beetle, which had become obsolete, and it, too, was a massive success, becoming the benchmark for mass-produced compact cars worldwide.

In 2005, the Golf underwent another model change for its fifth generation, and to showcase the new design, Volkswagen sponsored five JAF-sanctioned races at the Fuji, Motegi, Sugo, Okayama, and Mine circuits, using almost the same car body as that on the market.

There were nearly 30 entries in total across the three classes: the newest Model V, the older Model III, and the LUPO, which is the same size as the Model I Golf.

September 11, 2005 was a hot day. Automobile racing is already a very strenuous sport, but on this day, the track surface temperature was over 50 degrees Celsius, and the air was filled with the smell of tire rubber baking on the asphalt, brake pads burning at 800 degrees Celsius, and the smell of heated oil and fuel. The Mine Circuit is 3.3 km per lap and requires more frequent acceleration and deceleration than other circuits, which puts more stress on the drive and braking systems. It takes nearly an hour to drive the 30-lap 100 km race. I was confident in my physical strength from my daily swimming workouts, and unlike today, I was in pretty good shape back then, but the conditions were still a bit tough for a 46-year-old man like I was. My car was suffering from overheating, but if I didn't overtake the car in front, I'd be locked out of the podium.

In the latter half of the race, a faster Model V car came up behind me on a tight corner. I was used to driving on the Mine Circuit, so I decided to give way to the car on the straight ahead and held my line. Then, the car came into my line and hit the front of my car. There was a loud thump and rattle, and it felt like the entire structure of the car up to the front of the radiator had fallen out. "You idiot!" I exclaimed, but fortunately it didn't affect my driving and I was able to maintain my racing speed. I kept on accelerating, but the water temperature gauge stopped going up, and I caught up with the car in front of me in the same class, which I was having a hard time overtaking. My shadow loomed large in the driver's rearview mirror and I put pressure on him. He was in such a hurry that he made a mistake in decelerating before a curve, and spun out twice and careened off the course. As I dodged the spinning car, I shouted with joy, "Got ya!" I saw in my rearview mirror that the car had gotten back on the track and was now behind me. But my car was no longer overheating, so I continued on my merry way to the checkered flag and a podium finish in front of a large crowd of spectators. The driver who hit me came to apologize afterwards. I accepted his apology, and the race was over.

Now that the Mine Circuit is no longer available, I have been driving at the Autopolis International Circuit near Mt. Aso. It is considered a technical circuit and is 4.7 km long per lap. For a while, I participated in official races in a Honda Integra racing spec car, which cannot be driven on public roads. However, the official races were mentally and physically taxing, and in consideration of my age, I began to participate in "party races" that were less strenuous instead. I now compete in the Kyushu Challenge Cup Series in a red Mercedes-Benz C63AMG with the 6,208cc V8 DOHC engine. But I'm unable to show its true performance at Autopolis, a technical circuit with high output and heavy cars. When I finish the manuscript of this book and have more time, I would like to drive at Fuji Speedway, located at the foot of Mt. Fuji. This circuit has the longest straight in the world, and I believe that the C63AMG's performance can be fully demonstrated there. Perhaps on the straight stretch there my car would reach the takeoff speed of a B-29. Anyway, the Aso region in the center of Kyushu Island is scenic and full of wonderful inns offering many hot springs and delicious cuisine, and if you ever come to Japan, you should definitely stop by.

My book will likely not sell many copies due to its content. However, in the unlikely event that it sells well and I receive a decent amount of royalties, I would like to purchase a Chevrolet Corvette equipped with the latest mid-ship engine and drive it around Autopolis. I think that it'd be a perfect fit for that circuit. If there are any Corvette fans out there, show me your support!

I am deeply grateful to be able to enjoy a fulfilling sporting experience using the Earth's gift of fossil fuels, and in return, I want to do something that will bring joy to the Earth. I am sure that our planet is pained by the existence of nuclear weapons. I believe that writing a book like this one, which advocates for the abolition of nuclear weapons, is one way to repay the Earth for its kindness.

13. THE TINIAN —NAGASAKI—OKINAWA ROUTE

Tinian is an island of everlasting summer.

Countless B-29s once flew sorties from there to Japan.

Although there are differences in displacement and horsepower, all internal combustion engines share a similar design principle, and I know the smell that they emit in summer when being pushed to their limit.

The tension before a sortie. The rush of adrenaline during air-to-ground combat. The mental vacancy after returning safely.

As I have learned from motorsports, especially from official competitions, there is only one way to achieve goals in an arena that requires both the ability to make full use of modern machines and the technical support of mechanics: one must set a target early, assemble the best people available, and repeatedly and thoroughly experiment, adjust, and manage risks.

Why on Earth would the U.S. have even entertained multiple possible targets for a nuclear strike mission? Carrying it out required the most advanced technology of its time. It was funded at a cost of one third of the national budget. The only option was perfection!

This "multiple target" narrative must have been strategic information developed to deceive everyone - even the American people.

The story that Kyoto was considered as a potential target is particularly egregious. When I was in the fifth grade of elementary school, one of my teachers said to me in no uncertain terms, "America is truly virtuous. They recognized Kyoto to be a world treasure due to its many ancient historical sites, so they spared it from a nuclear attack."

I think that by 1943-1944, the target cities for the atomic bombings had already been decided. Both of them were large cities near the shipyards that built Japan's enormous Battleship Yamato, and the latter is near the shipyard that built Battleship Musashi. Of course, this may not be the only reason, but I believe that there must have been an emotional aspect to these targets for many Americans.

It is often said that air power was the decisive factor in deciding the outcome of the Pacific War, but I believe that for the U.S. Navy of the time, their battleships were the most highly prized. The fact that the signing ceremony for Japan's surrender after the Pacific War was held on board Battleship Missouri is proof of this. In 2015, Paul Allen, the co-founder of Microsoft, made global news when he announced that after investing significant time and financial resources into the effort, his team had located the sunken Musashi off the coast of the Philippines. Many Japanese still feel pride and nostalgia for having built the world's largest battleships, "Yamato" and "Musashi". I, too, am thrilled that the U.S. found the Musashi's remains!

The U.S. military must have carefully considered what sort of response there would be from the victims doomed to suffer the unprecedented atrocity of the nuclear bombings. They would have studied in detail the temperament, ideology, and sentiments of the people of each target metropolis, as well as the underlying religious conditions.

In the Hiroshima area, Jodo Shinshu is very popular. My understanding is that Jodo Shinshu is a religion in which the ultimate goal is to go to paradise (gokuraku-oujou) by maintaining one's faith until death.

On the other hand, in Nagasaki, the Urakami area, where 12,000 Catholics lived, was the hypocenter area. According to Catholic teaching, death is the separation of the spirit from the body, and at the end of the world, the body is resurrected and reunited with the spirit, which is then judged by God and enters eternal life.

By the way, a nuclear bomb can weigh as much as 5 tons, and the B-29, the pride of the U.S. military, dropped it from an altitude of about 9,000 meters at a speed of 300 kilometers per hour, where most Japanese anti-aircraft guns could not reach and fighter planes had poor interception capabilities.

In the case of Hiroshima, under clear skies and visible sighting conditions, the three-plane nuclear strike group was moving north when they turned west near Mihara City, 60 kilometers east of Hiroshima, and maintained a straight, level flight toward the city center. The pilots made fine adjustments to the Norden-type sighting device by inputting various data such as speed, direction, altitude, wind direction, wind speed, air pressure, and temperature etc. Then, the aircraft acquired the target, Aioi Bridge, 16 kilometers ahead, and pressed the drop switch at 5 kilometers ahead. Then, an elaborate arithmetic system (which we would now call a computer) was activated to make final adjustments, and 15 seconds later, the bomb suspension was automatically released and the bomb was dropped. The bomber, suddenly lightened by the loss in weight, rose several tens of meters in a moment, and in order to avoid the shock wave of the explosion, immediately made a U-turn to the right, accelerating to full speed in order to break away. The reason for the right turn was probably to reduce damage to the dropping aircraft by evacuating over the mountainous area to the north of Hiroshima City, which would have somewhat mitigated the shock wave from the plain. The bomb detached from the mother plane and fell at an initial speed of 300 km/h in a parabolic curve toward a target about 4 km away, exploding 44 seconds later near the Aioi Bridge at the designated altitude. (from "Countdown Hiroshima")

Even the slightest error in these processes could have resulted in an explosion that was many kilometers off target, in some cases, resulting only in the destruction of oceans and mountains, which are not strategic targets at all. Thus, drop targeting is a highly technical operation.

In the case of urban bombing, large bridges were often chosen as targets. This is because large rivers are clearly visible on the plains when viewed from above, and it is easy to find the target bridges by looking for the lines they make across the river.

The U.S. military demonstrated the destructive power of the nuclear bomb in the attack on Hiroshima, and would have been able to collect detailed data on the explosion over the plains.

After the successful detonation test of the plutonium bomb on July 16, from July 20 to August 8, a total of 42 bombs were dropped on various parts of Japan by visual or radar sight for data collection using a "pumpkin," a mock atomic bomb for bomb-dropping training, filled with about 2,500 kg of conventional explosives instead of a plutonium explosive device (from Mr. Kudo's and Mr. Okuzumi's book).

It is likely that the accuracy of visual sighting drops in clear weather was improved from these tests. However, considering the Soviet Union's severe weather conditions, defensive systems, and vast mountainous terrain, the U.S. military must have anticipated the need for nighttime radar targeting of military bases and strategic locations. In other words, if a nuclear attack on the Soviet Union was ever deemed necessary, visual sighting may not have been sufficient for success.

One of the main reasons for choosing Nagasaki was to investigate the impact of the shock waves of the bomb when dropped on a city surrounded by mountains.

Visiting the Nagasaki Peace Museum, I saw a large replica of the city of Nagasaki with a flashing display of the hypocenter, and the flashing was almost in the center of the Urakami area from Nagasaki Station, which stretched from north to south, surrounded by mountains. When I saw it during my visit, I was seized with a sudden thought: "The U.S. military must have been aiming at this spot from the very beginning."

14. URAKAMI CATHEDRAL

Perhaps the old Urakami Cathedral was always intended as the target. Stealth fighter planes, which are difficult to detect on radar, have a flabby, curved structure. Contrast that sort of shape with the Urakami Cathedral, which stood tall and angular on a small hill and would have looked like a huge, floating cross when seen from the sky. These characteristics may have made it easier to recognize on radar screens. However, if this is true, it may well still be top-secret information. We can only speculate.

I have been to various European cities and St. Petersburg, and many of them have a tall church rising in the middle of the city center with a sharply angled structure. A large church would make for a good nighttime radar target - and besides, a nuclear attack of any kind is already a godless act.

Of course, if it was true that the U.S. military had deliberately targeted the former Urakami Cathedral, it would have been a very controversial matter if the world were to find out. The cathedral is the largest Catholic holy site in Japan and is a place at which many Catholics were martyred. There were also many Catholics living in the surrounding area. It is obvious what would happen if it was discovered that a holy place and its believers had been deliberately targeted with a plutonium bomb. Therefore, the U.S. military invented a "fake scenario" in which the plutonium bomb had to be dropped in the area due to force majeure.

What was needed for this scenario was a "hypothetical first target city." The closest military city to Nagasaki is Kokura. Unlike Hiroshima, the U.S. military first bombed Nagasaki with only a few conventional bombs to make it appear as if it was not a priority target city. The Yahata Steel Works, about 10 kilometers from Kokura Arsenal, was made the target of a conventional bombing attack because it was a convenient target for launching a long-range raid from China to train the B-29 strategic bomber crews.

In order to increase the apparent tactical appropriateness of targeting Kokura with nuclear bombs given its expansive arsenal, it may have been designated a no-bombing zone in a deliberate effort to keep it preserved.

According to my patient's story, what was mainly being made in Kokura at the time were balloon bombs. Even if thousands of such bombs were to be dropped across the North American continent, they would have been little more than mosquito bites, and were not a threat from a tactical standpoint. Furthermore, as the U.S. military was anticipating the possibility of an engagement with the Soviet Union or its allies on the Korean peninsula, it may have wanted to preserve Kokura as a logistical support base for such an engagement. As a matter of fact, Kokura did play a significant role as a logistical support base for the U.S. forces in the subsequent Korean War. The tragedy that occurred in Kokura at that time was made into a novel by Seicho Matsumoto, titled "Tattoo on the Black Soldier's Breast"

Also, the U.S. military was treating strategic targets in this area as classified information by June 20, 1944. Kokura Arsenal is described as follows: "If we land in Kyushu, we have the advantage of 'local' production of arms and ammunition. The loss of this arsenal would mean that, in addition to logistical difficulties and transportation burdens, we would have to find alternative means to furnish supplies." In other words, "if the U.S. forces land in Kyushu in the future, they can occupy the Kokura Arsenal and use it as a local supply source of arms and ammunition, so we must not attack it." This document was dated June 20, 1945, before the Nagasaki Disaster.

Little information remains on the situation in Kokura during the Korean War (1950–1953). There must be many stories from this period that people may prefer not to connect to the present day. In particular, a large amount of weapons were produced at the arsenal. After being stored in the huge Yamada Ammunition Storage located near the arsenal, they must have been transported to the Korean Peninsula. The manufacture of these weapons must have brought about an unprecedented economic boom. Japan as a whole enjoyed a boom during the Korean War, but Kokura must have been especially prosperous because of the large amount of weapons it supplied to the conflict on the Korean Peninsula.

The Korean War ended with the tragedy of mutual massacres of fellow Koreans and the disastrous devastation of the entire peninsula. A long period of time has passed since then with no victory or armistice, just the two Koreas facing each other at the 38th parallel. It is truly a victim of the Cold War between the East and the West.

The artificial boundary of the 38th parallel was not decided upon by the people living on the Korean Peninsula. It was decided between the United States and the Soviet Union at the end of World War II, when Japan was about to surrender. Officially, on September 2, 1945, after Japan signed the Instrument of Surrender, MacArthur announced that the Soviet Union would disarm Japan north of the 38th parallel on the Korean Peninsula, while American forces would disarm Japan south of that line, as an order from the Supreme Command of the Allied Powers. The people of the Korean Peninsula had no part in this, nor did they dream of the division of their nation.

On August 9, the day of the Nagasaki bombing, Soviet forces declared war on Japan, and by August 15 had advanced to the northeastern part of the peninsula. Thereafter, they moved south to the 38th parallel, disarming surrendered Japanese troops.

An advance detachment of U.S. troops entered the Korean peninsula on September 6. They then disarmed the Japanese forces south of the 38th parallel.

On September 6, the "Preparatory Committee for the Establishment of the DPRK," which had already been formed, declared the inauguration of the "People's Republic of Korea" as an all-national government. However, the aspirations of the Korean people were ignored, and the U.S. and Soviet Union began their occupation of the country. Although Korea was a victim of Japan, it was not a defeated nation. However, the occupation marked the beginning of the tragic struggle between the two ethnic groups that divided the peninsula into two halves.

In December 1945, the foreign ministers of the United States, Britain, and the Soviet Union met in Moscow and issued the Moscow Declaration, which included the establishment of a provisional Korean government and a five-year trusteeship.

Those who had been demanding immediate independence launched a furious campaign against the trusteeship, and the cry for independence spread to both the north and south of the country. However, the Soviet military rule in the north and the U.S. military rule in the south created two opposing regimes.

15. THE PLUTONIUM BOMB

In the "Fat Man" era of plutonium bomb design, bringing a five-kilogram sphere of plutonium from subcritical to supercritical conditions necessitated the simultaneous (at near-millisecond precision) detonation of 64 directional explosive charges surrounding the sphere, themselves requiring a high voltage impulse to cause said detonation. The theory and structure behind this is too complex and elaborate for me to try to understand, let alone explain. However, in the book "Countdown Hiroshima," the author, Steven Walker, describes the Trinity test in Jornada del Muerto Desert, New Mexico on July 16, 1945.

IT WAS A strangely appropriate place to test the world's first nuclear bomb. A parched land largely inhabitated by jackrabbits and rattlesnakes and turkey vultures and a few forlorn ranchers scraping out a living until the bomb makers finally evicted them. Even its old Spanish name was appropriate: the Jornada del Muerto, it was called. The Dead Man's Journey.

The author appears to have conducted extensive research, so I'm inclined to find his descriptions credible. The following is a quote from his book describing the scenery just before the atomic explosion.

> *AT ZERO minus five minutes, a short siren blast wailed across the desert. Seconds later, a green rocket flared up into the sky.*
>
> *Through the loudspeakers, the hollow strains of Tchaikovsky's Serenade for Strings mingled with Sam Allison's countdown. Voice of America's early*

morning classical music show was now in full swing.

All over the Jornada, radiation monitors sat at their shelters or in their trucks, listening to the countdown over the radio. Soldiers detailed to supervise possible evacuations smoked last cigarettes as they waited outside lonely desert towns. Cameraman and photographers made final adjustments to their equipment, polishing lenses, checking exposures with their flashlights. To the east, over the Little Burros, the faintest gleam of light was now discernible. Dawn was not far away.

Outside the control bunker at S10,000, armed guards sat in jeeps, their motors idling, ready to evacuate the scientists at an instant. Inside the bunker, Don Hornig stared at a control panel in front of him. There were four lights on it. Right now, they were all blank. Exactly forty-five seconds before zero, his colleague Joe McKibben would throw the switch closing the automatic timing circuits for the bomb. Once Hornig saw his four lights go red, he would know the X-unit was charged, ready to disgorge its five and a half thousand volts to the bomb's sixty-four detonators. After that, if anything went wrong, the only way to stop the bomb from blowing up was to cut power to the X-unit.

Next to Hornig was a knife switch controlling the power. He figured he had perhaps half a second to react if there was a problem. Half a second to abort the world's first nuclear bomb. It was enough to make anyone a little crazy. He turned to Oppenheimer and made a joke. "What's likely to happen, Oppie," he said, "is that at minus five seconds I'll panic and say—Gentlemen, this can't go on—and then I'll pull the switch."

For a long moment Oppenheimer stared at him. "Are you all right?" he asked.

At zero minus two minutes, the siren wailed again, a slow, stretched howl that seemed to hang forever in the desert air.

At zero minus one minute, a red rocket spat up into the sky. It was 0528.

Philip Morrison, the man who ferried the bomb's care all the way from Los Alamos, hunkered down on the ground. The camp looked like a place of the dead. Shadowy bodies lay everywhere, immobile and silent. It felt as if everybody was collectively holding his breath, waiting for whatever it was out there by the tower and the sweeping searchlight to do its worst. Morrison wondered what the worst would be. Tonight was the test, at best a beautiful, brilliantly conceived scientific experiment. In just a few days, perhaps, it would be the real thing. Morrison was not the only scientist who almost wished the bomb would fail. Like many, he was caught in a trap of desire and horror. The physicist in him wanted to see the experiment succeed. The human in him wanted to see it fail. Sometimes, like Leo Szilard, he even questioned whether it was necessary at all. Now the threat of a Nazi bomb had disappeared, its purpose was uncertain. The only certainty was that the power they were about to release in the next minute would change the world forever.

Forty-Five seconds before zero, exactly on cue, Joe McKibben pulled the switch triggering the automatic timing sequence. All the circuits to the bomb now closed. Don Hornig stared at his panel, waiting for the four red lights to glow. Right behind stood Kistiakowsky, looking over his shoulder. His entire reputation, not to mention month's salary, now rested on whether the troubled X-unit would finally work. Hunched against the racks of equipment to their left was Thomas Farrell, the general who felt the plutonium core in his rubber gloves two days earlier. A First World War veteran, all he could think of now was how much worse this was than going over the top. Over in base camp, General Grove's very last thought was what would happen if the countdown got down to zero, and nothing happened.

The red lights on Hornig's panel flicked on. The X-unit was energised and ready. His eyes glued to the panel. His hand still rested on the knife-switch, waiting for the word to abort. Allison's countdown passed the ten-second mark. Everybody in the shelter braced himself. Farrell noticed how Oppenheimer barely breathed. In the last moment he suddenly grasped a beam, as it to steady himself. Somebody heard him murmur, "Lord, these affairs are hard on the heart."

And then, in the final seconds before zero, a strange noise filled the air. Only later the men who were there learned what it was. It was the noise of frogs, hundreds and hundreds of them, mating in the dawn. They had come up from the surface after the long night of rain, slipping into the cool, sandy puddles. In the instant before the bomb ripped open the sky, the only sound in the desert was the sound of life in the act of creation.

Fifty miles north of Ground Zero, and eighteen-year-old girl was traveling in the front seat of a car next to her boter-in-law, Joe Willis. The girl's name was Georgia Green, and Joe was driving her to an early-morning music lesson in Albuquerque. They still had some way to go. As the passed the town of Lemitar along an empty Highway 85, a flash of extraordinary brilliance suddenly filled the landscape. Georgia grabbed her brother-in-law's arm. "What was that?" she cried.

Joe stared at her. Georgia Green was blind.

Once the X-Unit charge switch was flipped, the nuclear reaction began. In the Trinity test, the X-Unit charge switch was activated 45 seconds after it was fully charged, which instantly produced the world's first nuclear explosion.

The Trinity test was observed from a laboratory 10 km away from the actual detonation. While the X-Unit and the charger themselves must have been with the bomb itself, there must have been some kind of remote operation in order to conduct the test - but the window for activation would have been small once the X-Unit was charged. The author does not get into any specifics on this part of the story, so I can only guess that, perhaps, the details remain U.S. military secrets.

The detonation of the plutonium bomb required the simultaneous electrical stimulation of the 64 directional explosives around the core, all at 5,500 volts. Once the necessary electrical capacity was reached, a device called the "X-Unit" was used to distribute the electrical charge to the explosives. On the flip of a switch, electric current flowed into the X-Unit, and four lights turned red in succession to indicate when the charge was ready. If current to the X-Unit was switched off at this point, the X-Unit lost the ability to distribute the electrical charge. In other words, the bomb could not be easily recharged.

That said, with the technology of the time, if the charge switch was not turned on within a few minutes, the X-Unit lost its capacity to reliably distribute its charge. Considering the expense involved in the bomb and the mission, rather than risking the possibility of a failed drop, it seems quite a bit more likely that bombers would have been instructed to return to base in the event of a complication.

Both the X-unit and the charger would have been installed in the bomb casings and remotely operated from the aircraft by specialists, who would have had to work closely with the bombers to ensure that the charging of the bomb was complete within a few minutes of it being dropped. In the case of Nagasaki, the charge switch was linked to the altimeter and set to charge the explosives at an altitude of 500 meters.

Assuming that this is true, it would have been impossible to arm the plutonium bomb and then fly around and around over Kokura for 30 minutes.

Now, if the bomb had been aimed at the Urakami Cathedral, it managed to detonate within 500 meters of the target, proving that advanced radar sighting technology had reached an accuracy equivalent to clear-day visual sighting. However, radar sighting technology was top-secret at the time, and with the war against the Soviet Union in mind, it would have been impossible to say that radar had been used, even if one was able to discuss the bombing at all. The order for the pilots to use only visual sighting to confirm the target was likely a fabrication that was issued after the nuclear bombs were dropped.

Unlike the uranium bomb dropped on Hiroshima, the plutonium bomb had a complex and elaborate structure, and a very elaborate procedure was required to prepare for the drop on the plane, charge the "X unit," and detonate it. Naturally, details on the procedures have remained top-secret to this day, but the technology of the time would have required various detailed protocols to be followed for the device that enclosed and detonated the plutonium, such as for heating components and wiring before detonation, oil management, etc. Therefore, I believe that while the plutonium bomber stayed over Yakushima Island to prepare the bomb for drop, another two planes from Mariana Islands circled over Kokura at a low altitude of 3,000 meters, as if they intended to bomb Kokura. When the preparations for the explosion were complete, the bomber plane with the other two planes probably headed for Nagasaki, increasing altitude in a northwesterly direction. However, if all three planes flew together at an altitude of 9,000 meters, as they did at Hiroshima, they would have been noticed, so they remained separated by a considerable distance. The first plane dropped the measurement device by parachute over Nagasaki and headed south. The second plane, after dropping the nuclear bomb, fled to the northwest, then turned to the East China Sea and flew south. The third plane would have approached the mushroom cloud after the blast had subsided, taking photographs as it, too, headed south.

The fuel tanks would have needed to be increased in order to return to Tinian, as the aircraft consumed a considerable amount of fuel in the process from takeoff to drop preparation. However, such a modification would not have been possible for a B-29 carrying a heavy and dangerous nuclear bomb. Therefore, I believe that Okinawa was chosen from the beginning as the return destination after the nuclear attack on Nagasaki.

Yes, Okinawa.

The nuclear strike team left Tinian, dropped a nuclear bomb on Nagasaki, and landed on Okinawa, marking the opening of the post-war scenario for Japan that the U.S. military had planned.

In the Pacific War, the U.S. military invaded from two directions to defeat Japan. One was the Nimitz Line from the Marianas to Iwo Jima, and the other was the MacArthur Line from the Philippines to Okinawa. The B-29s took off from Tinian, dropped a plutonium bomb, a weapon of the new era, and landed in Okinawa - a critical strategic location for the U.S. after Japan's defeat in their resistance against both the Soviet Union and continental China. This moment raised the curtain on a new American battle for world domination.

The U.S. invested tremendous military power, material resources, and technology to build this Tinian–Nagasaki–Okinawa route. The return of B-29s to Okinawa after their nuclear attack cemented the U.S.'s position as the world's top military power and put in motion the occupation and colonization of Okinawa. Above all, this choice would have made a strong impression on the U.S. military's own soldiers. It was truly the first step towards the U.S.'s goals, as the first redrawing of the maps in a post-World War II world.

All of the issues with the U.S. military base in Okinawa, and the Northern Territories that have been occupied by first the Soviet Union and then Russia, began here.

The path that Japan must take towards the abolition of nuclear weapons requires rejecting the theory of nuclear deterrence and waking up from the insanity of tolerating such weapons at all. Specifically, Japan must remove itself from the U.S. nuclear umbrella, and as a truly independent nation, upgrade its Self-Defense Forces and engage in national defense with a greater sense of urgency and a strategically oriented mindset.

Currently, there is a debate about the need for Japan to strengthen its military in response to Russia's invasion of Ukraine, but I believe that it is important for Japan to first make unambiguously clear that its military exists exclusively for defense. A constitutional debate will be necessary for this; at the very least, Japan should clarify in the Constitution that it will not develop or possess nuclear weapons. Any increase in the military budget should be considered only after that.

At the same time, by making sincere diplomatic efforts and enriching private-sector exchanges, Japan should aim to be respected by non-nuclear weapon states and nuclear weapon states alike, including the U.S., Russia, China, and North Korea, as a country that rejects the theory of nuclear deterrence. This is also the shortest path to a true resolution on the Northern Territories and Okinawa issues.

In order to achieve this, it is necessary for each and every Japanese citizen to have the strong determination and courage to abolish nuclear weapons, informed by a sober understanding of global affairs.

16. WHAT HAPPENED TO THE RUINS OF URAKAMI CATHEDRAL?

Infinite sorrow
Eternal warmth

When I first saw the image of Christ in "The Last Supper" with my wife, I felt enveloped by an indescribable gentle light. His expression is one of infinite and profound sorrow for human folly, with a warm smile that shows an eternal faith in the goodness of humanity, in their potential to turn that folly around.

To be clear, I am not a Christian.

What appeals to me about the image of Christ in this famous painting by Leonardo da Vinci is that it differs from conventional paintings of Christ. It strikes me as a powerful expression of some universal cosmic divinity arising from da Vinci's own personal beliefs; he merely borrowed the image of Christ to communicate it.

The Church of Santa Maria delle Grazie and the Dominican Monastery in Milan, where The Last Supper is installed, were both severely damaged by multiple direct hits from conventional bombs aimed at the city during World War II. Miraculously, however, the destruction did not affect the mural of The Last Supper.

As I stared at the mural, I thought of the remains of the former Urakami Cathedral that survived a direct hit from a plutonium bomb, which had a destructive power incomparable to the bombs that hit Milan. The remaining wall, which was a cross-shaped pillar of the Grand Cross structure, was pushed off a few centimeters from the foundation by the pressure of the bomb, but somehow managed to remain standing. The wall of the building stood tall, like a huge mural in its own right, and the statues of St. John and Our Lady of Sorrows standing close to it had a beautiful, even deep expression.

The mural of The Last Supper was in danger of destruction many times in the past, but the reason it survives today is due to the presence of people who had a strong will to preserve it. Their will has a strength that can withstand a direct hit from a bomb.

In contrast, the Atomic Bomb remains of Urakami Cathedral, which was meant to be an irreplaceable monument to convey the truth of the bombing, underwent demolishment starting on March 14, 1958, despite the opposition of numerous preservation movements, including the Nagasaki City Committee for the Preservation of Atomic Bomb Materials. Except for a small portion of the wall, which was moved to another location, the ruins were destroyed, and a new Urakami Cathedral was built on the site.

If the remains of the old Urakami Cathedral had survived to the present day, it would have held spiritual value as a symbol of Nagasaki on par with, or surpassing, the Atomic Bomb Dome of Hiroshima, and could have stood as a testament for the whole world to the threat of nuclear weapons. Why? Because the remains of this building were a crystallization of the blood of many Christians martyred in Nagasaki and other cities: such remains could have conveyed the depths of the nuclear attack as the ultimate persecution of Christians in Japan.

From the Edo period to the early Meiji period (1614–1873), the Urakami area was under the control of the Edo shogunate. During this period, there were four incidents of suppression of Christians that occurred there, referred to as the "Urakami Kuzure." The word "kuzure" originally referred to "roundups," but two of these incidents, the "First-kuzure" of 1790 and the "Second-kuzure" of 1842, ended without much violence due to a lack of evidence. In the "Third-kuzure" of 1856, an informant's tip-off triggered the martyrdom of several dozen Christian leaders. The "Fourth-kuzure" of 1867, however, involved a large-scale prohibition of Christianity at the end of the Edo shogunate at a completely different level of suppression from the previous ones, culminating in the martyrdom of 3,394 residents of Urakami. The Meiji government, which followed the Edo shogunate, intensified the persecution of Christians even further, torturing exiles to an unspeakable degree. Ultimately, under heavy criticism from other Christian countries, the Meiji government declared a halt to the suppression in 1873, and the situation was brought to an end. By this point, 664 people had been martyred.

The old Urakami Cathedral was a Romanesque-style "house of god" built on the site of a village headman's house, where fumi-e (treading on religious icons), a method used to determine whether a person was a Christian or not, was once practiced. The red bricks were built one by one over a period of 30 years by people who inherited the faith in the area, pooling their funds and labor in their simple lives in memory of the hardships of their forefathers. The building area is 1,163 square meters, or about 3 acres. The tower was said to be the largest church in the East, reaching a height of about 30 meters.

The building was in the shape of a cross that was too large to be noticeable from the ground, instead becoming visible only when seen from the sky. That is to say, it was visible only to God and the birds - and human pilots.

The plutonium bomb that hit Nagasaki exploded at a height of 500 meters above the city, at a point 500 meters away from the cathedral.

The NHK Special that was broadcast on August 18, 2014, "The Unknown Shockwave—The Threat of the Mach System," claimed that the U.S. military had set the bomb to explode at about 500 meters above Nagasaki based on precise advance calculations. The altitude of the explosion was set so that the shock wave would be transmitted to the ground. They already knew that at that altitude, the shock wave would be most efficient—most destructive—if impelled into a wide area on the ground. As calculated, the most intense shock wave would be generated at 500 meters from the hypocenter. In other words, the former Urakami Cathedral stood in the area of maximum destructive power of the plutonium bomb. That portion of the building that was able to survive the bomb was like the solidified spirit of the precious bonds of the congregation of Urakami Cathedral, who expressed their respect for the Catholic martyrs that died there with each and every red brick that built the building. Perhaps it was these believers' souls that stood in the way of the shockwave. According to the calculations of the U.S. military, the former Urakami Cathedral was likely expected to get completely destroyed. The fact that it survived in spite of this must have been seen as an event not easily explained by scientific calculation alone.

17. DR. NAGAI

This is the quote from the book by Dr. Nagai that was referenced earlier.

I have heard that the second atomic bomb, calculated to deal a deadly blow to the war potential of Japan, was originally destined for another city. But since the sky over that city was covered with clouds, the American pilots found it impossible to aim at their target. Consequently, they suddenly changed their plans and decided to drop the bomb on Nagasaki, the secondary target. However, yet another hitch occurred. As the bomb fell, cloud and wind carried it slightly north of the munitions factories over which it was supposed to explode, and it exploded above the cathedral.

This is what I have heard. If it is true, the American pilots did not aim at Urakami. It was the providence of God that carried the bomb to that destination.

Is there not a profound relationship between the destruction of Urakami and the end of the war? Urakami, the only holy place in all Japan—was it not chosen as a victim, a pure lamb, to be slaughtered and burned on the altar of sacrifice to expiate the sins committed by humanity in the Second World War?

Dr. Nagai's thinking here is better understood with some background. The oppression that Urakami Village suffered due to its large Catholic population (roughly half of residents) began to subside after the Meiji Restoration of 1868, and was incorporated into Nagasaki City in 1920. However, there were ongoing conflicts with the old city center, which still followed the Japanese syncretic religion of combined Shintoism and Buddhism. A dynamic emerged in which the anti-Catholic community argued that the atomic bomb was dropped on "Urakami," not on "Nagasaki," and that the bombing was the divine punishment of God of Shinto because the Catholics did not pray at Shinto Shrine of Suwa. These people claimed that the residents of Urakami must show their thanks to the Christian God, as they were chosen to atone for the sins of mankind.

As a radiologist, Dr. Nagai had been suffering from leukemia since before the atomic bombing, and after the bombing on August 9, he worked for three days as the leader of the 11th Medical Corps of the Nagasaki Medical College as a relief worker. He then evacuated his two children to Mitsuyama, located northeast of Nagasaki City. On September 25, his right carotid artery, which had been severed in the atomic bombing, opened again, causing severe bleeding. Combined with his leukemia and the overwork of his sleepless relief work, he fell critically ill. However, he miraculously recovered thanks to the prayers of his children and the generous care of those around him. On October 15, he prepared a "Report on the Rescue Activities of the 11th Medical Corps" and submitted it to Nagasaki Medical College. On November 23, at a joint funeral for the atomic bomb victims held in front of the remains of the Urakami Cathedral, he delivered a eulogy under the name "Takashi Paul Nagai, representative of the Urakami faithful of the Tenshukyo Church." Although he was in a weakened state at this point, it is evident that he had reflected deeply on the situation given the complexity of the thoughts he expressed in it. Nonetheless, he did not mention the "first target Kokura theory," which strongly indicates that he had not heard about it.

He then began writing a novel, "The Bells of Nagasaki" which he finished in August 1946, but the publication was suspended by the Occupation Forces Command, and the manuscript was sent to the U.S. Department of Defense. Nagai's idea that the atomic bombing of Nagasaki was an act of divine providence caught the attention of the U.S. military establishment. At the time, the U.S. military was extremely strict in its control of information and speech, especially with regard to Hiroshima and Nagasaki, and the manuscript of "The Bells of Nagasaki" must have been thoroughly scrutinized. As a result, the U.S. military center must have come up with the idea that Nagai's ideas could be used. If the Nagai Idea spread, it would pave the way for thought control, forcing the victims to accept as "divine providence" the greatest atrocities in the history of human warfare: the dropping of nuclear weapons on a civilian center. The delay in publication was likely caused by the military's preparation to spread this idea freely while hiding the influence of the U.S. military as much as possible.

The attribution of the atomic bomb to divine providence would have gone a long way toward maintaining the morale of the U.S. occupation forces themselves. Many of the American soldiers who entered Nagasaki after the bombing must have felt a deep sense of guilt about what their troops had done when they were exposed to the unspeakable power of the atomic bomb. This must have been especially true for the lower-ranking soldiers who had to deal with the situation on the ground. The fact that a Japanese doctor, who had himself been exposed to the atomic bomb, spoke of the atomic bomb as a blessing from God that would redeem all mankind may have gone a long way toward keeping the American soldiers at that time under control.

According to Seiichi, his eldest son, Dr. Nagai became almost bedridden due to the worsening of his leukemia, but based on his strong Catholic faith, he believed that it was his duty to spread the horror of the atomic bomb that took away his beloved wife in an instant, and he wrote with unspeakable patience and spirit. During the day, people came to visit him one after another to console him in admiration for his intelligence and personality, so he wrote at night.

"His red blood cell count was 2 million (normal range–5 million), white blood cell count was 280,000 (normal range -7,000), had a fever of about 37-38 degrees Celsius, and suffered from anemia, swollen spleen, abdominal fluid, hemorrhoidal bleeding, bleeding from gums, nose bleeds, and pale complexion. We met most of the visitors who came to visit my father in his illness, but he would frequently say that what he wants most is 'time and rest.'"

As a clinician, I wonder how he managed to maintain his composure in such a state. Without very strong mental fortitude, a person would normally have broken down under such stress.

I speculate that a high-level American military intelligence officer may have interacted with him and told him that Kokura was intended as the primary target. Based on this information, Dr. Nagai added to the manuscript of his eulogy for the joint funeral of the atomic bomb victims held in front of the remains of Urakami Cathedral, which he then turned into a novel. The novel was finally approved for publication in 1949 at the request of the occupying forces, along with "The Tragedy of Manila," a book describing the atrocities systematically committed by the Japanese military.

In his own introduction to "The Bells of Nagasaki" at the time, Dr. Nagai wrote the following:

The purpose of this book is to spread the actual situation about the atomic bomb and to inspire people to dislike war and protect peace. Thinking from that point, I am grateful that the occupation forces who have given us a record of Manila and started to publish it as a combined book, which will be a very positive effect.

In an unsigned preface to "The Tragedy of Manila," a writer wrote the following:

If a man were to suddenly go on a rampage and kill anyone and everyone he meets on the street, the police must restrain him. This is the task that Japan assigned to the U.S. - the whole world. In order to end Japan's indiscriminate killing, in order to put an end to the war, the U.S. - the whole world - had no choice but to use atomic bombs. By doing so, they were able to save countless lives, not only in Japan, but in other countries as well.

The war that Japan started in 1937 at Voromizo Bridge and in 1941 with the deliberate surprise attack on Pearl Harbor finally turned back onto Japan, ending with the complete destruction of the cities of Hiroshima and Nagasaki.

Reading passages such as these, we can feel the weight of the times that Dr. Nagai struggled to describe, under labored breath and with a feeble right hand, pressing down upon us. The loyal subjects of a King of Terror that scorched Japan, indiscriminately bombing Japanese cities one after another, culminating in the dropping of two nuclear bombs, descended upon Nagasaki and tore through the rest of the country, repressing the flow of information, all in the name of being the "world's police."

It is particularly important to emphasize that the many photographs documenting Hiroshima and Nagasaki in the immediate aftermath of the bombings were not made public at all. There must have been numerous records of the countless ashen corpses and bodies lying in heaps perhaps much larger than those seen in the Nazi extermination camps. These photos would have revealed the scale of the bombings as unprecedented atrocities, but they were uniformly confiscated. The only images we have today are those showing destroyed artifacts and a small number of bombing victims and bodies. Perhaps more explicit photographs are available somewhere, but I have not been able to find them.

If you read "Atomic Cover-up" by Greg Mitchell, which describes the extent of the information control under GHQ, you will be stunned at just how thorough it was, both over the Japanese and their own citizens. At the time, one must have been left with the bizarre impression that the U.S. had developed and deployed the nuclear bombs in some kind of superhuman manner.

Given these circumstances, I am in awe of the brilliance of Dr. Nagai's mind, which overcame the censorship of the U.S. military to publish his numerous masterpieces. I, along with my wife, are among the doctors involved in community medical care in Kokura. If Dr. Nagai was the first to insinuate his suspicion of the "first target Kokura" theory, I am honored to succeed him in offering my own researched thoughts.

I quote again from the eulogy in the novel, "The Bells of Nagasaki."

Is there not a profound relationship between the destruction of Urakami and the end of the war? Urakami, the only holy place in all Japan—was it not chosen as a victim, a pure lamb, to be slaughtered and burned on the altar of sacrifice to expiate the sins committed by humanity in the Second World War?

This statement has been the subject of much debate in the years that followed.

In 1972, the poet and atomic bomb survivor Yamada Kan criticized Dr. Nagai in the monthly magazine "Ushio," writing that "Dr. Nagai's explanation is nothing more than complicity in concealing the anti-human principles inherent to the very concept of atomic bombing. It is nothing more than demagoguery that reinforces American political ideas intended to deflect and dampen the unquenchable resentment of the people." In the 1980s, the writer Hisashi Inoue wrote, "According to Nagai's explanation, one might be able to insist that the U.S. use of atomic bombs was a righteous act... but by invoking the providence of God, humanity is spared from taking responsibility for its actions. No explanation could be more convenient for a tyrant."

The magnum opus of Nagai criticism came in 1994, when Professor Shinji Takahashi of Nagasaki University published a book entitled "Philosophy in Nagasaki: Death and Life in the Nuclear Age." Here is an excerpt:

In his "Urakami Holocaust Theory," Takashi Nagai asserts that the atomic bombings were God's "great providence" and does not hold the Japanese ruling class responsible for the war or U.S. leaders responsible for dropping the bombs. This is an extremely convenient narrative for such authorities. For the Japanese and U.S. ruling class in charge of the postwar process, the Urakami Holocaust Theory, which does not even suggest that either party was responsible for starting the war or for dropping the atomic bombs, was a concept worth promoting for political reasons. And promoted it was - far beyond the intentions of Takashi Nagai. In Nagai's own words, a lone "laboratory man" had been "elevated as the new face of the publishing world."

Certainly, in Professor Takahashi's framing, the logic holds.

However, it is important to remember that Dr. Nagai lived in a time when the Occupation Forces were oppressively restrictive of speech and writing. It is also true that, in spite of these conditions, Dr. Nagai had things that he wished to write, and there were many Japanese who could find encouragement in reading what he wrote.

In this context, I would like you to read the following quote again, which I first quoted at the beginning of this chapter:

I heard that the second atomic bomb, calculated to deal a deadly blow to the war potential of Japan, was originally destined for another city. But since the sky over that city was covered with clouds, the American pilots found it impossible to aim at their target. Consequently, they suddenly changed their plans and decided to drop the bomb on Nagasaki, the secondary target. However, yet another hitch occurred. As the bomb fell, cloud and wind carried it slightly north of the munitions factories over which it was supposed to explode, and it exploded above the cathedral.

This is what I have heard. If it is true, the American pilots did not aim at Urakami. It was the providence of God that carried the bomb to that destination.

Note that it says, "This is what I have heard." As only those who dropped the atomic bombs, i.e., those in the U.S. military, would have had any information about the bombings, we can surmise that he is referring to a story told by the Occupation Forces. And note the following phrase, "If it is true." In other words, if "what [he had] heard" was not true, the narrative he proposes, which is so convenient for the U.S., would be fundamentally thrown into question. For Dr. Nagai, who was almost bedridden and on death's door, it was impossible to confirm the truth of the story he was told by the U.S. military—but it seems that he harbored misgivings about it, at the very least.

It is also noteworthy that the novel deliberately adds the phrase "the American pilot did not aim at Urakami." In the manuscript of the eulogy of November 1945, this part was written as "the fact is that the atomic bomb, which was aimed at the center of Nagasaki City near the prefectural office, was deflected to the north due to the weather and fell directly in front of the Urakami Cathedral." It did not contain the words "aim at Urakami."

By casually emphasizing "did not aim at Urakami," Dr. Nagai may have actually sensed the psychological maneuver by the U.S. military to conceal the fact that it had targeted Urakami Cathedral or something else in the Urakami area for the bombing.

Simply speaking, if it is not true, the American pilots would have aimed at Urakami.

Perhaps this is the message that Dr. Nagai intended to leave for posterity, managing to slip it through the censorship of the U.S. military.

What follows is a quote from the novel "Chains of the Rosary."

The third day. The student casualties had been taken care of, and I returned home in the evening. Nothing but a patch of burnt ash. I quickly found it. A black mass, after reaching the kitchen. --It was a pelvis and lumbar vertebrae, still there amidst the burnt-out ruins. Nearby was a rosary chain with a cross on it.

I picked up my wife and put her in the burn bucket. The remains were still warm. I held her to my chest and went to the grave...in my arms, my wife was making the dry, crumbling sound of phosphate lime. I heard it as her saying, "I'm sorry, I'm sorry."

The following is a quote from the novel "Leaving My Child Behind"

I was dozing off, and before I knew it, Kayano came back from playing and pressed a cold cheek on mine, saying after a while, "Ahhh... this is Dad's smell." Must I soon leave this world—and leave this child behind? Having long forgotten her mother's smell, can she not at least know her father's? This adorable little girl, who sneaks up on me in my sleep? Does she know that his mother was lost in the fires of war, and that although his father's life was ultimately spared, even he will soon be gone as well?..."

We who live today should learn from Nagai's spiritual strength, which kept its brightness and inspired people's hope in the face of a vicious fate: losing one's wife in an atomic bombing, suffering from his own radiation exposure and weakening as he passed away, leaving behind two children, all in the midst of the Occupation Forces' severe control of the public discourse.

18. DATA BASED ON THE HIROSHIMA AND NAGASAKI NUCLEAR TESTS

This section contains a large table, as can be seen below.

Pentagon's Estimated Bomb Requirements for Destruction of Russian Strategic Areas, September 1945

Surely, you understand what this table shows.

The first column contains the name of a city in the USSR.

The next column contains the area of that city, in square miles.

The final column is the number of plutonium bombs calculated as necessary to destroy the city.

Already by September 1945, the U.S. military center had calculated that if 204 bombs were dropped on all 66 cities, all of the Soviet Union's strategic bases could be destroyed.

Moscow, located on a wide plain, was 110.0 square miles at the time and would have taken six bombs to destroy, while Leningrad, which is surrounded by mountains and was 40.4 square miles at the time, would also require six. Do you know what this means?

These calculations were made possible by interweaving data on the atomic bombing of Hiroshima, which was located on a broad plain, with data on Nagasaki, which is surrounded by mountains. This alone seems to be sufficient to conclude that the U.S. never intended to target Kokura at all. Calculations such as these would not have been possible based on data obtained from a bombing of Kokura, which, like Hiroshima, is located on a relatively large plain.

City	Area of City in sq. miles	No. of Bombs
Moscow	110	6
Leningrad	40.4	6
Tashkent	28.9	6
Baku	7	2
Novosibirsk	22	6
Gorki	13.5	4
Sverdlovsk	20.2	5
Chelyabinsk	11.5	3
Tbilisi	12.7	3
Omsk	6.6	2
Kuibyshev	12.6	3
Kiev	64.4	6
Lvov	20	5
Kazan	20	5
Alma Ata	13.1	4
Kharkov	30.1	6
Riga	40	6
Saratov	8.8	2
Koenigsberg	37.8	6
Odessa	28.7	6
Rostov-on-Don	14.4	4
Dnepropetrovsk	9.2	3
Stalino	7.1	2
Yaroslavl	14.1	4
Ivanovo	16.2	4
Archangel	11	3
Khabarovsk	10	3
Tula	8.1	2
Molotov	5.7	2
Astrakhan	4.8	1
Magnitogorsk	10	3
Vladivostok	10	3
Stalingrad	20.3	5

City	Area of City in sq. miles	No. of Bombs
Ufa	10.8	3
Irkutsk	11.5	3
Vilna	20	5
Voronezh	17	5
Izhevsk	7.5	2
Chkalov	10.2	3
Grozny	1.3	1
Stalinsk	10.8	3
Nizhni Tagil	17.3	5
Penza	5.8	2
Minsk	4.2	1
Kirov	5.3	2
Tallinn	16	4
Kemerovo	5	2
Ulan Ude	22.3	6
Komsomolsk	5	2
Murmansk	4	1
Belostok	6	2
Vitebs	3.9	1
Zlatoust	5.6	2
Makhach Kala	1.8	1
Syzran	5.4	2
Chimkent	13.4	4
Batum	3.9	1
Kovrov	1.8	1
Orsk	4.8	2
Kamensk	4	1
Brest Litovsk	4.5	1
Sterlitamak	3.1	1
Ishimbaevo	4	1
Neftedag	4	1
Ukhta	4	1
TOTAL-66 CITIES	901.3	204

The very idea of destroying a city is insanity. I shudder just looking at these numbers.

As a psychosomatic physician, I intend to continue my work in better understanding the atomic bombings of Nagasaki and Hiroshima. It is how I can do my part in confronting the global madness of so-called "nuclear deterrence."

19. PRESIDENT OBAMA'S VISIT TO HIROSHIMA

The following is a quote from the opening of Remarks at Hiroshima Peace Memorial by President Obama, who was the first sitting president to visit Hiroshima, on May 27, 2016.

Seventy-one years ago, on a bright, cloudless morning, death fell from the sky and the world was changed. A flash of light and a wall of fire destroyed a city and demonstrated that mankind possessed the means to destroy itself.

Why do we come to this place, to Hiroshima? We come to ponder a terrible force unleashed in a not so distant past. We come to mourn the dead, including over 100,000 in Japanese men, women and children; thousands of Koreans; a dozen Americans held prisoner. Their souls speak to us. They ask us to look inward, to take stock of who we are and what we might become.

"Death fell from the sky" has the nuance of a catastrophe that fell from the sky unprompted. This is identical to the post-war psychological framing that was discussed previously that treated the inescapably man-made act of dropping a nuclear bomb seem like a natural disaster. That said, this does not damage President Obama's achievement in his visit to Hiroshima.

Perhaps the U.S. military itself, which dropped the two atomic bombs, is deeply aware of how atrocious and inhumane it really was. While they may have tried to justify the bombings with the insane logic of "nuclear deterrence," the Soviet Union (now Russia) resisted; now, the number of nuclear powers has increased to nine, and there are stockpiles of nuclear weapons all over the Earth with destructive power more than 1,000 times greater than the plutonium bombs dropped on Nagasaki. The range and targeting accuracy of the missiles are also so high that they are simply incomparable to those of the days when bombs were dropped from B-29s. About five years before the invasion of Ukraine, a video of Russian President Vladimir Putin boasting, "The performance of our nuclear weapons has gotten even better!" made international news. Why are the people of the world not horrified by such a news report? Do they not realize that such an announcement is, from a psychological perspective, extremely abnormal?

While everyone knows that nuclear weapons are heinous, they continue to exist because people still do not comprehend their true horror. The nuclear powers have succeeded in manipulating information by exploiting the psychological influence of nuclear weapons in a variety of ways. The very existence of nuclear weapons has already deeply affected the way that people think and the 'truths' that they accept.

Intimidation through force.

The horrors that lurk in the depths of the human psyche.

As a result, threatening behavior is rampant in homes, schools, companies, organizations, and even in the world of hobbies. Many people have been hurt from such behavior—some of them, in fact, are patients at my clinic.

Accepting the existence of nuclear weapons results in embracing the nature of a society willing to do so.

But even today, if a nuclear weapon were to be detonated somewhere, not all the doctors in the world would be able to prevent the vast hellscape that it would cause.

While both I and my wife work on the front lines of infectious disease control as medical practitioners, using the same standards as all of our colleagues, the challenges posed by nuclear weapons are on a completely different level. Infectious diseases affect people's minds and bodies, while nuclear weapons affect people's souls. Accepting the absolute evil of these weapons in order to protect one's own country is a stain on one's dignity and way of life. Many people are unaware of this.

I am a follower of Buddhism.

The Nirvana Sutra, a Buddhist scripture, teaches that "if you are killed by an evil elephant, you shall not go to hell—but if you approach evil hypocrite, you shall go to hell, indeed." In ancient India, elephants were given alcohol to make them drunk, and then released into crowds to kill or injure large numbers of people in combat. Thus, an evil elephant is a weapon for indiscriminate attacks, and in modern times, the ultimate "evil elephant" is the nuclear weapon. In the process of doing good, we should not be intimidated by the threats and persecutions of such hard power, even if they sometimes lead to death.

On the other hand, "evil hypocrite" refers to nefarious people who infiltrate people's souls with words that instill a disregard for life, sowing despair and discontent, all under the guise of saintly intent. The philosophical claim that the Sutra makes, then, is that one must always exercise extreme caution to identify and avoid such evil hypocrite.

20. NUCLEAR PARALYZED JAPANESE

In September 2014, a friend of mine, a city councilor, brought up my arguments expressing doubts about the First Target Kokura theory as a general question at a regular meeting of the Kitakyushu City Council. As a result, the mayor of Kitakyushu promised two things: to interview citizens about the situation on August 9, 1945 and to send a researcher to the U.S. National Archives and Records Administration.

This resulted in a collection of citizen testimonies about the Yahata Air Raid of August 8, 1945; in 2017, a researcher was dispatched to the U.S. National Archives as well.

Furthermore, the mayor of Kitakyushu City came to the commemoration of the publication of my book "Revive The Bells of Nagasaki!" in 2019.

Then, partly at my insistence, the Kitakyushu City Museum of Peace was opened in April 2022 by the city council. The site is right next to where the replica of the "Nagasaki Bell" was enshrined. Yet, the "motto" of the museum as a whole is that Kokura was the primary target of the nuclear bombings and that Kokura's existence is significant in this regard in the museum's emphasis on the preciousness of peace.

In other words, the arguments I provide here had been discarded.

The problem is not that my arguments were not accepted, but that I had no opportunity to speak up and engage in dialogue in the museum construction project, which was initiated by my efforts.

I want to make a final request. If there are any American citizens who agree with my position, I pray that they might wade through the oceans of documents in the National Archives and publish any evidence that shows that Kokura being the "first target" was never anything more than a strategic false narrative.

This may be the only way to prove the truth, and I can only hope for such assistance.

The Japanese government would not even participate as an observer at the Conference of the Parties to the Nuclear Weapons Convention held in Vienna this past June. The House of Councilors election, the national election in July, was focused on economic issues, and nuclear abolition was hardly mentioned at all. What do the people of the world think of this?

In Japan today, we are experiencing unusually hot summers, heavy rains causing rivers to overflow and landslides, heavy snow disasters, earthquakes, large typhoons, tornadoes, and other disasters more frequently than before. Global warming may be a factor, but perhaps the heavens are angry and saddened by the current situation in Japan.

21. A RELIGION OF RIGHTEOUSNESS

Dr. Nagai concluded his novel "The Bells of Nagasaki" with the following words:

> *"With the nuclear power he has acquired, mankind now possesses the key to his own destiny. This is truly a shuddering thought, for I feel that only a religion of righteousness can be trusted with such responsibility."*

What did Dr. Nagai, a Catholic, mean by writing "religion of righteousness" instead of "Christianity"?

In March 1971, at the urging of my aunt, I joined Sōka Gakkai at the age of 11. Sōka Gakkai is the largest Buddhist organization in Japan and now has members in 182 countries around the world. That same year, I went to Nagasaki on a school trip and was exposed to the reality of the atomic bombing, which proved to be a formative moment in my life.

At that time, the world was in the midst of the so-called "Cold War," with the U.S. vying for supremacy with the Soviet Union and China. However, a confrontation had erupted between the Soviet Union and China, both of which were in the communist camp. The U.S. took advantage of this situation to restore diplomatic relations between the U.S. and China—over the head of its close ally, Japan—under the leadership of Deputy Chief of Staff Henry Kissinger. While he also did much to restore relations between the U.S. and the Soviet Union, he was unable to resolve the Sino–Soviet conflict, and the threat of nuclear war between the Soviet Union and China grew.

It was in this context that Daisaku Ikeda, the third president of Sōka Gakkai, released the "Japan–China Proposal" in 1968, which called for the hastened normalization of diplomatic relations with China. This was done in accordance with the "Declaration Against Atomic and Hydrogen Bombs" (see the Appendix at the end of the book), the legacy of Josei Toda, the second president of Sōka Gakkai. While this was met with a storm of criticism in Japan, it made waves throughout the world. And indeed, at that time, Daisaku Ikeda, the founder of the opposition party Komeito cooperated with the governing Liberal Democratic Party, under the leadership of Prime Minister Kakuei Tanaka normalized diplomatic relations between Japan and China in 1972. Next, Daisaku Ikeda visited the Soviet Union in September 1974 and met with Prime Minister Kosygin, who promised that the Soviet Union would not launch a preemptive attack on China. In December 1974, he visited China and met with Premier Zhou Enlai, Deng Xiaoping, and other leaders to convey Kosygin's promise.

As we know, nuclear war did not ever break out between China and the Soviet Union.

In 1975, Dr. Kissinger, then Secretary of State, invited Daisaku Ikeda to a meeting. Their ongoing friendship resulted in a collection of talks entitled "Dialogue On Peace, Life, and Philosophy."

In retrospect, while the desperate efforts of members of Soka Gakkai in Japan to expand their teachings led to antipathy toward the organization among many people at that time, their activities proved to hold world-historical significance. After all, Daisaku Ikeda's "Japan–China Proposal" had a significant impact not only in Japan and China, but also in the world, and he had frequent close meetings with the leaders of various countries, despite being a private citizen. Behind these efforts was his position as leader of Sōka Gakkai, which at the time boasted a membership of 10 million households and was a supporting body of the Komeito, the third largest party in the national political system. He was able to use this huge membership base as the foundation for the movement against nuclear war.

Next, I will introduce a waka poem in Japanese. This is a waka poem that Daisaku Ikeda personally wrote and gave to me when I was a young doctor in my thirties and still just starting out.

権力は魔性なりせば快活に 若き利剣で見事破れや

Here is the meaning of the above Japanese sentence.

All that power is
devilishness itself
So, in lively fashion,
the sharp edge of youth must rise
and shatter it to pieces

For a long time, I did not understand the meaning of "power" in this poem.

I finally realized, after the age of 60, that the ultimate "power" in this world is the threat of nuclear weapons.

This book is the result of my modest but lively attempt to shatter the spell of that mighty power with my own sharp edge.

Hopefully, each and every member of Sōka Gakkai International, both in Japan and in its 192 member countries around the world, will renew their commitment to the abolition of nuclear weapons. I also hope that the Komeito Party, founded by Daisaku Ikeda and currently in a coalition with the Liberal Democratic Party, will begin to advocate for the abolition of nuclear weapons more strongly than it does now, rather than speak about economic issues alone.

APPENDIX 1

Declaration Against Nuclear Weapons

By Josei Toda, second president of Soka Gakkai on September 8, 1957 at Mitsuzawa Stadium in Yokohama

Today's "Festival of Youth" has been blessed with clear, sunny skies free of any trace of yesterday's storm, as if the heavens themselves have responded to your enthusiasm. With a great feeling of joy, I watched the competitors among you display the Soka Gakkai spirit in each event, as the rest of you wholeheartedly applauded their efforts.

Nevertheless, for all the joy I feel today, it is inevitable that Soka Gakkai will encounter persecution again. I am also fully prepared to meet any attack that comes my way personally. Having said that, I would now like to share with you what I hope you will regard as the first of my final instructions for the future.

As I have long said, the responsibility for the coming era will be shouldered by the youth. There is no need for me to tell you that *kosen-rufu* [spreading the value of respect for life] is our mission. We must absolutely achieve it. But today I would like to state clearly my feelings and attitude regarding the testing of nuclear weapons, a topic that is now being debated heatedly in society. I hope that, as my disciples, you will inherit the declaration I am about to make today and, to the best of your ability, spread its intent throughout the world.

Although a movement to ban the testing of nuclear weapons is now underway around the world, it is my wish to attack the problem at its root, that is, to rip out the claws that are hidden in the very depths of this issue. Thus I advocate that those who venture to use nuclear weapons, irrespective of their nationality or whether their country is victorious or defeated, be sentenced to death without exception.

Why do I say this? Because we, the citizens of the world, have an inviolable right to live. Anyone who tries to jeopardize this right is a devil incarnate, a fiend, a monster. I propose that humankind applies, in every case, the death penalty to anyone responsible for using nuclear weapons, even if that person is on the winning side.

Even if a country should conquer the world through the use of nuclear weapons, the conquerors must be viewed as devils, as evil incarnate. I believe that it is the mission of every member of the youth division in Japan to disseminate this idea throughout the globe.

I shall end by expressing my eager expectation for you to spread this first appeal of mine to the entire world with the powerful spirit you have shown in today's sports festival.

The Background to this Declaration

Soka Gakkai's second president Josei Toda (1900–1958) used the occasion of a Soka Gakkai youth division sports festival to make it public, but what gave rise to the thoughts in the declaration was his two-year incarceration during World War II, when, together with first president Tsunesaburo Makiguchi, he was imprisoned by Japan's military government for what were then considered subversive thoughts: opposing war. At the time he chose to announce his declaration, Mr. Toda was troubled by the thought that his time was limited as his own life was nearing its close. He chose to leave this declaration as his final will to the youth division members and, through them, to the world.

A word of explanation is in order concerning his use of the word literally translated in the declaration as "devil". In speaking from the Buddhist point of view, "devil" refers to those tendencies existing within human life itself that, when set in motion, sap people's life force and torment the human heart and mind. The epitome of this destructive function is, in Mr. Toda's thinking, nuclear weapons. When Mr. Toda called for execution of anyone using nuclear weapons, he was not thinking in terms of legislating an actual death penalty. He chose those words as the clearest way to vilify the devilish function within human nature that attempts to justify the use of nuclear weapons.

At the opposite pole from the devilish functions existing in human life is a life brimming with compassion and creative force. If the one may be called the functioning of a "devil", then the other may be called the functioning of a "Buddha". As long as the Buddha function—the human capability for inventiveness imbued with compassion—exists, then a way can be found to abolish nuclear weapons. This was Mr. Toda's conviction.

APPENDIX 2

Bring the stream of peace with the power of dialogue
Poet Laureate Daisaku Ikeda

World peace
is not something that is given.
It is something human beings create
with their own power and wisdom.
Without the struggle for human revolution
to identify one's mission
and enhance it,
there is no peace.

We must fight to put an end to the nuclear age.
But not against the nuclear weapons,
the nuclear powers,
or nations that develop them.
What we must confront and overcome,
Is 'the mindset that accepts nuclear weapons'
—the willingness to destroy the opponent to fulfill one's desire.

The power of dialogue
is what brings the world together.
It is by dialogue that we can find clues,

to solve the growing number of global-scale problems.
Without dialogue, humans will wander in a darkness called self-satisfaction.
Dialogue is a light in the darkness
that sheds light on the road ahead one
another and helps find the path to take.

Buddhist teachings overcome all differences.
It stands on life, the most universal foundation.
There, freeing one from narrow and
generally accepted ideas and prejudices—
connecting heart-to-heart, life-to-life, boldly but sincerely,
and opening a way for the creation of mankind's new values.
It is to move. To speak.
Each tireless wave,
from "separation" to "unification,"
"opposition" to "friendship,"
"war" to "peace."
Believing that it becomes the stream to
change the history of the human species.

APPENDIX 3

SGI President Urges G7 Leaders to Move toward "No First Use" of Nuclear Weapons at Hiroshima Summit

Daisaku Ikeda is a peacebuilder, Buddhist philosopher, educator, author and poet. As third president of the Soka Gakai lay Buddhist organization in Japan, founding president of the Soka Gakkai International (SGI) and founder of several international institutions promoting peace, culture and education, he has dedicated himself to bolstering the foundations of a lasting culture of peace.

On April 27, 2023, SGI President Daisaku Ikeda issued a statement calling on the leaders of the G7 countries meeting in Hiroshima from May 19-21 to take bold steps toward resolving the conflict in Ukraine and guarantee the security of all humanity by taking the lead in discussions on pledges of No First Use of nuclear weapons.

Mr. Ikeda, an ardent proponent of nuclear weapons abolition since the 1960s, sees the G7 Summit in Hiroshima as a chance to build on the unwavering activism of the hibakusha—survivors of the Hiroshima and Nagasaki nuclear bombings—and their determination that the tragic impacts of nuclear weapons never be experienced again.

He states: "As the G7 leaders revisit the actual consequences of the nuclear weapon detonation and the bitter lessons of the nuclear era, I urge that they initiate earnest deliberations on making pledges of No First Use so that their shared recognition of the inadmissible nature of the nuclear weapons can find expression in changed policies."

He warns that with the taboo against the use of nuclear weapons being eroded among the nuclear-weapon states, and frameworks for managing and reducing nuclear arsenals verging on collapse, there has never been a greater need to establish policies of No First Use.

Regarding Ukraine, Mr. Ikeda urges that the Hiroshima Summit should provoke a "prescription for hope" by working for an immediate cessation of attacks on civilian infrastructure and developing concrete plans for negotiations that will lead to a cessation of hostilities.

He stresses that representatives of civil society, such as physicians and educators who protect people's lives and futures, should join such negotiations as observers.

Mr. Ikeda references the work of the physicians, Dr. Bernard Lown and Dr. Yevgeny Chazov, from both sides of the Cold War who founded IPPNW (International Physicians for the Prevention of Nuclear War) in the early 1980s and met in Hiroshima under the slogan: "Let us Live Together, Not Die Together." In the same spirit, he concludes with the vital need to shift to a "common security" paradigm for all humankind.

This is the third time in the past year that Mr. Ikeda, a veteran advocate for nuclear weapons abolition, has called for No First Use policies. He first pushed for declarations of No First Use in 1975, following visits to prominent leaders and thinkers in all five declared nuclear-weapon states.

Read the full statement on 'DAISAKU IKEDA WEBSITE'.

[Adapted from an April 27, 2023, press release of the International Office of Public Information, Soka Gakkai, Japan] All from DAISAKU IKEDA WEBSITE.

https://www.daisakuikeda.org/

AFTERWORD

When I was a sophomore in high school, I visited the United States by myself.

Unlike today, the process to enter the U.S. back then was rather arduous, but thanks to the efforts of my parents and many other people, I was able to experience a 10-day homestay in Alameda, a city south of San Francisco.

Coming into contact with the size of the U.S. and the kindness of the people there resulted in a significant expansion of my sense of the world.

As a college student, the Sōka Gakkai International Japan–US Joint Youth Division General Meeting at the San Diego Sports Arena was an experience that has had a profound impact on my life.

I also have fond memories of attending an international conference in Orlando, Florida during my doctoral program. Disneyworld is massive and I found it to be a really interesting place. I will never forget the steak I enjoyed with researchers from many different countries.

At the International Space University Summer Session in Huntsville, I had a great time not only with my American friends but also with my Russian and Chinese friends.

As I mentioned earlier in the book, I would love to someday drive the latest Chevrolet Corvette on the Autopolis International Circuit in Aso, Japan.

I wrote this book in the sincere hope that the United States will abolish its own nuclear arsenal and be reborn as a truly prosperous, beautiful, and compassionate country.

As I am writing this, I have just come across a report of an intensified missile attack by Russia on Kiev. How heartbreaking. Someday, when peace comes to Ukraine again, I would like to travel to Kiev and other parts of Ukraine. I deeply hope that that day will come as soon as possible.

I wish to express my gratitude to the many doctors that offered support during my presentation on the unknown aspects of the Nagasaki bombing at the 22nd World Congress of International Physicians for the Prevention of Nuclear War (IPPNW) held at the University of York, UK, in September 2017, including IPPNW Japan Branch Representative Branch Director Yoshitake Yokokura, Branch Director Keiichi Hiramatsu, and Vice Branch Director Masao Tomonaga. I also wish to thank Dr. Katsuko Kataoka, Dr. Susumu Shirabe, Dr. Takashi Kojima, and Secretary General Kazuko Kamikouchi, for their warm encouragement during my poster presentation at the Japan Chapter General Assembly in May 2018.

On August 6, 2022, the 77th anniversary of the atomic bombing of Hiroshima, IPPNW senior Dr. Umeyo Yunokawa invited me to be a guest singer at the No more Wars & No more Hiroshima's / Nagasaki's Concert starring her in Hiroshima. The concert was held in a concert hall with a beautiful night view and I sang two songs, Georges Moustaki's 'HIROSHIMA' and Nagasaki singer-songwriter Masaharu Fukuyama's 'KUSUNOKI', and had a wonderful time with 100 people. I would like to express my deepest gratitude to all of you. I am deeply grateful to excellent soprano Miyuki Shirakawa and well-known singer Yuko Uno for training me carefully.

I would also like to thank my good friends Tomonori Akiyama, Jun-ich Yasunaga, Dr. Yoichi Kawano and Saburo Nakao for their heartful support.

Thank you also to Soka Gakkai members Kiyohiro Azuma, Eiji Ohnishi, Dr. Takashi Yagyu, Hiromi Nakatomi, Dr. Shunsuke Nakatomi and Akutagawa Prize Winner Kiyoko Murata for their soulful encouragement.

Also, I am extremely thankful to Yumi Itabashi of One Peace Book Inc., and the translator Thomas S. Evans.

Finally, my deepest thanks to my wife Naomi, whose beauty, intelligence, and kindness are my source of inspiration and motivation, and to my other family member, Anne, my Welsh Corgi dog, who watched over me as I wrote.

Thank you very much.

I respectfully dedicate this book to former Mayor Iccho Itoh.
May peace be with you all.

Notes on Chapter 7

In Chapter 7, I have appended Notes because of the lengthy citations in general.

7. John Hersey, HIROSHIMA (Snowball Publishing, 1993), p18-19First published in New Yorker, August 31, 1946

7.1 THE NEW YORK TIMES, AUG. 9, 1945: Website The article was written by W. H. Lawrence, who is different from the following W. L. Laurence.

7.2 William Leonard Laurence of the New York Times, WINNING WORK; September 8, 1945, Atomic Bombing of Nagasaki Told By Flight Member: Website by source provided in the 1946 Pulitzer Prize Winner display.

7.3 Kitakyushu City Museum of Peace English translation of the text that was posted as of August 2022 in the building

7.4 Takashi Nagai, The Bells of Nagasaki, Translated by William Johnston, Nagasaki Nyoko no Kai 2022—first published 1949, p165–167

7.5 Akinaga, Yoshiro, Munehiro, Hiroshi, The History of the Pacific War, Junior Edition, Peace Edition, "Atomic Cloud Waku", Shueisha, 1962, p238–241.

7.6 Peter Townsend, The Postman of Nagasaki, William Collins Sons & Co. Ltd, 1984, p59–60

7.7 Vice Admiral Frederick L. Ashworth USN (Ret.), The Second Atomic Bombing Nagasaki Shipmate, September 1987, p18 (A further important...)), p19 (Take off for the lunch...)), p20 (It was decided that...)

7.8 Maj. Gen. Charles W. Sweeney, U.S.A.F. (Ret.) with James A. Atonucci and Marion K. Atonucci, WAR'S END An Eyewitness Account of America's Last Atomic Mission Avon Books, 1997, p193–194 (I had already decided...)), p202 (He expressed disappointment...)), p148 (As we had practiced,...)), p198 (We were reminded...)), p210 (At 30,000 feet,...), p213–215 (Kokura lay ahead....)

7.9 Frederick L. Ashworth, The Second Atomic Bombing Nagasaki, p20–21 (As we laid our course...)

7.10 Charles W. Sweeney with James A. Atonucci and Marion K. Atonucci, WAR'S END, p216–218 (I couldn't believe my eyes,...)

WORKS CITED (in order of appearance in the text)

English Language Publications

1) Pilot's Flight Operating Instructions for Army Model B-29 Airplanes, Periscope Film LLC, 2006

2) Lesley M. M. Blume, FALL OUT-The Hiroshima Cover-up and the Reporter Who Revealed It to the World, Simon & Schuster, 2020

3) THE 509TH REMEMBERED, A History of the 509th Composite Group as Told by the Veterans that Dropped the Atomic Bomb on Japan, Robert and Amelia Krauss 2009

4) Takashi Nagai, The Bells of Nagasaki, Translated by William Johnston, Nagasaki Nyoko no Kai 2022—first published 1949

5) Peter Townsend, The Postman of Nagasaki, William Collins Sons & Co. Ltd, 1984

6) Vice Admiral Frederick L. Ashworth USN (Ret.), The Second Atomic Bombing Nagasaki Shipmate, September 1987

7) Maj. Gen. Charles W. Sweeney, U.S.A.F. (Ret.) with James A. Atonucci and Marion K. Atonucci, WAR'S END An Eyewitness Account of America's Last Atomic Mission Avon Books, 1997

8) Joseph Rotblat & Daisaku Ikeda, A QUEST FOR GLOBAL PEACE Rotblat and Ikeda on War, Ethics and the Nuclear Threat, I. B. TAURIS 2007... Quoted in chapter 10

9) Andrew Robinson, EINSTEIN—A HUNDRED YEARS OF RELATIVITY, Palazzo Editions Limited, 2005... Quoted in chapter 10

10) Greg Mitchell, Atomic Cover-up: Two U.S. Soldiers, Hiroshima & Nagasaki and the Greatest Movie Never Made, Sinclair Books 2012
11) Daisaku Ikeda, The Human Revolution 2, with a foreword by Arnold J. Toynbee, John Weatherhill, 1974
12) Stephen Walker, SHOCKWAVE—COUNTDOWN TO HIROSHIMA, HARPER PERENNIAL, 2006...Quoted in chapter 15
13) Paul Ham, HIROSHIMA NAGASAKI, BLACK SWAN, 2012... p591–593 Quoted in chapter 18
14) Susan Southard, NAGASAKI LIFE AFTER NUCLEAR WAR, VIKING, An imprint of Penguin Random House LLC, 2015
15) Harold Willens, THE TRIMTAB FACTOR: How Business Executives Can Help Solve the Nuclear Weapons Crisis, William Morrow and Company, 1984
16) Arnold Toynbee, Daisaku Ikeda, CHOOSE LIFE: A DIALOGUE, Oxford University Press, 1976
17) Aurelio Peccei, Daisaku Ikeda, BEFORE IT IS TOO LATE, Kodansha International, 1984
18) Rene Huyghe, Daisaku Ikeda, DAWNFTER DAEK, Weatherhill, 1991
19) Linus Pauling, Daisaku Ikeda, A Lifelong Quest for Peace: Dialogue, Jones & Barlett Learning, 2000
20) Mikhail Gorbachev, Daisaku Ikeda, MORAL LESSONS OF THE TWENTIETH CENTURY: GORBACHEV AND IKEDA ON BUDDHISM AND COMMUNISM, I.B.Tauris, 2005
21) Daisaku Ikeda, Transforming Human History: The Light of Peace and Dignity (47th Peace Proposal, 2022), Website

Publications in Japanese

1) Etsuko Kawashima, Ino Zu de Yomigaeru Ancient Dream, Nagasaki Kaido, Zenrin, 1997
2) THE HISTORY OF JAPAN, Shogakukan, 1993
3) Nagasaki Shimbun News Department, Cut it out! Violence: Nagasaki Mayor Shot Dead, Nagasaki Shimbun, 2008
4) Yoshiro Akinaga, Hiroshi Muneta, Junior Edition: Pacific War History, Peace Edition, Atomic Cloud Waku, Shueisha, 1962
5) Fujio Hironobu, Nagasaki Kaido Machiisha Fuzei (Part 1) —Silence in Kokura—Kitakyushu Municipal Medical Journal Kitakyushu Medical Journal, No. 635, 2010
6) Kagawa Eiki, War Diary of a Medical Student, Bungeisha, 2016
7) Association for Supporting Local Memory Heritage, What Happened in Yahata That Day: 70 Years after the Yahata Air Raid—A Legacy of Words by Those Who Experienced It 2015
8) Yozo Kudo and Yoshishige Okuzumi, U.S. Military Material, Air Raid in Kitakyushu: A Record of Incendiary Air Raids on Yahata, Moji, Okayama, Sasebo, and Nobeoka, Kitakyushu War Records Society 2002
9) U.S. military material, Yahata Steel Works Air Raid, Record of the first air raid on the Japanese mainland by B-29s, Kitakyushu War Documentation Society 2000
10) Kudo, Yozo, and Okuzumi, Yoshishige, The Drop: A Complete Record of the Side that Brought About Hiroshima and Nagasaki, 2005
11) Kudo, Yozo and Okuzumi, The Tinian File Tells of the Atomic Bombings: A Collection of Coded Telegrams, Self-published 2002
12) Akiyoshi, Miyako, Operation Atomic Bombing from the Side, Akiyoshi Miyako, Genshu Shuppansha, 2006
13) Matsumoto, Seicho, Tattoo on the Black Soldier's Breast, Shincho Bunko, 1965

14) Kimata, Jiro, Nihon Senkan Senshi (Military History of Japanese Battleships), Tosho Shuppansha, 1983

15) Masayasu Hosaka, Japan Atomic Bomb Development Secrets, Shinchosha Bunko 2015

16) Yamada Katsuya, How Nuclear Weapons Work Kodansha Gendai Shinsho 2004

17) Bruno Tertrais: ATLAS MONDIAL DU NUCLEAIRE, Japanese Edition, Nishimura Co.

18) Tetsuo Hashida, The Idea of Strategic Bombing: Guernica, Chongqing, Hiroshima Gaifu-sha, 2006

19) Hironobu Fujio, Naomi Fujio, Satoshi Dobara, Urakami Sixth Collapse: Resurrection of the A-bombed Maria, Doujinshi Kyushu Writers No. 129, 2015

20) Photo Book Uragami Tenshudo Catholic Uragami Church 1999

21) Nagami Shinpei, Nagasaki Goban Kuzure, Godo Shuppan 1975

22) Tsuyoshi Takase, Nagasaki: Another "Atomic Bomb Dome" that Disappeared, Heibonsha 2009

23) Yokote, Kazuhiko, Nagasaki Urakami Cathedral, 1945–1958: An Atomic Bomb Relic Lost, Iwanami Shoten, 2010

24) Catholic Urakami Church, The Story of "Journey"—Urakami Yonban Collapse, 2005

25) Takashi Nagai, The Bells of Nagasaki; Manila Tragedy and Gobon, Bensey Co. 2009 (first published 1949)

26) Tetsuro Konishi, The Original Manuscript of Takashi Nagai's Funeral Address at a Mass for the victims of the Nagasaki Atomic Bomb, The Journal of Nagasaki University of Foreign Studies No. 18, 2014

27) Takashi Nagai's Funeral Address at a Mass for the victims of the Nagasaki Atomic Bomb on display at the Nagasaki-City Nagai Takashi Memorial Museum.

28) Seiichi Nagai, Nagasaki no Kane wa Hohoemu: Chronicle of a Brother and Sister Left Behind, Seiichi Nagai, Josei Paulo Kyokai, 1995.
29) Nagai Takashi, Leave This Child, Sao Paulo (first published in 1949)
30) Shinji Takahashi, Philosophizing in Nagasaki; From Atomic Death to Peace Responsibility, Hokuju Publishing Co.
31) Shinji Takahashi, Philosophizing in Nagasaki; From Atomic Death to Peace Responsibility 2, Hokuju Publishing Co.
32) Iccho Itoh, Omoshiro Jittai Seijigaku: Chihousai 27.5 Yumezukuri (Interesting Politics of Reality: Local Government 27.5 Dream Building), Iccho Itoh Supporters Association, 2002
33) Yutaka Watanabe, The Nagasaki Atomic Bombing of a 15-Year-Old, Iwanami Shoten, 2002
34) Daisaku Ikeda, The Complete Works of Daisaku Ikeda, Vol. 145, The Human Revolution 4, Seikyo Shinbunsha, 2012, p368, quoted in Chapter 14
35) Henry Kissinger, Daisaku Ikeda, Dialogue On Peace, Life, and Philosophy, Ushioshuppansha, 1987
36) Norman Cousins, Daisaku Ikeda, A Dialogue toward Global Harmonization: Peace, Humanity, and the United Nations, Mainichi Newspapers, 1991
37) Hironobu Fujio, Revive The Bells of Nagasaki!, Gentosha, 2019

ABOUT THE AUTHOR

Hironobu FUJIO

Hironobu Fujio was born in 1959 to a paramedic father and a knitting teacher mother in Hakata Ward, Fukuoka City, and graduated from Shuyukan High School and Yamaguchi University School of Medicine. He currently runs an internal medicine, pediatrics, and psychosomatic medicine clinic with his wife in the Kokurakita Ward of Kitakyushu City. He also serves as a nursery school doctor, school doctor for elementary and junior high schools, and medical doctor for the Autopolis International Circuit.

He and his wife also perform "Wave of Joy" concerts in the waiting rooms of clinics, at civic centers, and at the Kitakyushu Performing Arts Center, etc. He is vice-chairman of the Kitakyushu Grand Philharmonic Orchestra. His hobby is playing the flute, and his favorite is the Russian composer Tchaikovsky.

As a member of Soka Gakkai and the International Physicians for the Prevention of Nuclear War (IPPNW), he is always looking for ways to further his advocacy for the abolition of nuclear weapons. He enjoys swimming, horse riding and social dance for health and exercise.